T0253094

Praise for

Still Life at Eighty

"*Still Life at Eighty* is a little jewel box of a book, full of epiphanies that are comforting and merciless in the gentlest possible way. Both a series of meditations and a user's manual about growing old. I was amazed by its clarity and very grateful to read it."

—Stephen King

"It's so very rare for a memoir to tell the naked truth about aging—its terrors and its treasures, its indignities and its mysteries. Who else but Abigail Thomas to lift the veil and show us how she is navigating her eighties. Here she is, sitting still in her chair, traveling on a river that flows both ways—backward slowly on the tides of memory, forward at a fast clip onward toward the open ocean. And sometimes, because of friends, because of dogs, because of children and home, writing and a wisteria vine, time stands still, and life is life, Abigail is Abigail, and once again we get to marvel with her, wonder with her, laugh and cry and rage with her."

—Elizabeth Lesser,
author of *Cassandra Speaks*

ALSO BY ABIGAIL THOMAS

Getting Over Tom

An Actual Life

Herb's Pajamas

Safekeeping: Some True Stories from a Life

A Three Dog Life

Thinking about Memoir

Two Pages

What Comes Next and How to Like It

STILL LIFE AT EIGHTY

The Next Interesting Thing

ABIGAIL THOMAS

SCRIBNER

New York   London   Toronto   Sydney   New Delhi

Scribner
An Imprint of Simon & Schuster, LLC
1230 Avenue of the Americas
New York, NY 10020

This Scribner trade paperback edition November 2024

SCRIBNER and design are trademarks of Simon & Schuster, LLC

Simon & Schuster: Celebrating 100 Years of Publishing in 2024

For information about special discounts for bulk purchases, please contact Simon & Schuster Special Sales at 1-866-506-1949 or business@simonandschuster.com.

The Simon & Schuster Speakers Bureau can bring authors to your live event. For more information, or to book an event, contact the Simon & Schuster Speakers Bureau at 1-866-248-3049 or visit our website at www.simonspeakers.com.

Interior design by Yvonne Taylor

Manufactured in the United States of America

10   9   8   7   6   5   4   3   2   1

Library of Congress Cataloging-in-Publication Data

Names: Thomas, Abigail, author.
Title: Still life at eighty : the next interesting thing / Abigail Thomas.
Description: Scribner trade paperback edition. | New York : Scribner, 2024.
Identifiers: LCCN 2024029506 (print) | LCCN 2024029507 (ebook) |
ISBN 9781668054659 (trade paperback) | ISBN 9781668054666 (ebook)
Subjects: LCSH: Thomas, Abigail. | Authors, American—20th Century—Biography.
Classification: LCC PS3570.H53 B Z46 2024 (print) | LCC PS3570.H53 B (ebook) |
DDC 813/.54—dc23/eng/20240701

LC record available at https://lccn.loc.gov/2024029506
LC ebook record available at https://lccn.loc.gov/2024029507

ISBN 978-1-6680-5465-9
ISBN 978-1-6680-5466-6 (ebook)

for my family

STILL LIFE
AT EIGHTY

Introduction

Pushing eighty, the future is behind me; the past is unpredictable; I am living in the ever-shifting constancy of now. Sometimes the present is interrupted by a memory so vivid that I am in two places at once, an inexpensive, unpatented, readily available form of time travel. These are the moments in which past and present are fused. I like to imagine them as little paperweights, holding my life together before it all blows away.

I write to find out what the back of my mind is doing while I'm doing nothing. I write to find meaning when meaning is hard to come by. I write through confusion for clarity. I write for fun. I have productive times when I wake up giddy and in gear, curious to find out where I'm headed, and lackluster times when I don't or can't write at all. Times when it is hard to have faith that the next thing will appear—the next interesting thing—and there seems no point to being me. I've been at this long enough to know there will always be the next thing, but I need an open mind. Sometimes it shows up in disguise, a bug, say, or a particular shade of blue, a joke somebody made that wasn't funny. And when I feel that tug, especially if it makes no sense, I pay attention. Because you never know.

PART ONE

BEING THIS OLD

Maybe the greatest miracle is memory.
—Brian Doyle, *One Long River of Song*

Written on My 40th Birthday, 1981

When I am old and fat and gray
all shoulder, rump, and rib cage
unable to move any more than this tub
can, I trust someone will hunch
over me with a blue sponge
and attend to my surface as I
am attending to the streaky outside
of this tub, this substantial curvaceous
unerotic old mother of a tub

and not fuss at me, or ask me
what my memories are, not expect me
to smile or sigh, because I will be
beyond all that, I will have earned
the right to keep still, not murmur
endearments unless they are part
of the job, part of the rhythm
of the work (good old girl,
you are a good old girl)

and if this sprucing up is ritual
so much the better, since I
have always been just surface
everything I know I have always known
first with my skin. And when
company is coming and you want
to look your best, battered is noble,
and worn out and beat up
and still able to hold water is honorable

When It Struck Me

SITTING WITH THE DOGS, drinking coffee, listening to the weather. Snow out there. "Wind chill warnings for today and tomorrow," says the reporter. "Most at risk, children and the elderly." At first the word "elderly" conjures up someone thin, frail, someone I might help across a busy street. Someone else. A moment passes before I realize, with a jolt, that I'm elderly. I don't feel elderly. I feel like myself, only more so.

The word I hate the most is "seniors." I was a senior once, but it was a long time ago, and I graduated. The label sounds condescending, all of us lumped together with lots of discounts and no identities, more like a marketing tool than a bunch of individuals. Given my druthers, I would rather be referred to as an elder. "Elder" brings with it the suggestion, no, the near certainty of hard-won wisdom. There are cultures who revere their elders but ours is not one of them. We seem to do everything to deny, even reverse, aging—and death? Death should remain out of sight.

I don't mind "old." I've been around long enough to call a spade a spade. At seventy-nine, a little overweight, plopped in a chair, I have never been so at home in my body. I like this age. I choose my clothes for color and comfort. No more tight sweaters and short skirts. No more sucking my stomach in when I go out. I never look in a three-way mirror. I never ask questions like "Do these earrings make me look fat?" Years ago I caught sight of myself in a good light, seeing far too much rouge, clunky bits of eyeliner, and lipstick elsewhere than my mouth. I reminded myself of my mother, whose cheeks got pinker and shinier with every passing year. I attributed this to her failing eyesight and I bought myself a magnifying mirror, so as to never leave the house again looking like an old lady clown. I washed my face and took a look. It was like traveling to another country. An unfamiliar but interesting topography that turned out to be my face. I've done a lot of laughing, and it shows. I've done a lot of everything, and it shows. I put my makeup away. Might as well look like who I've gotten to be. It took long enough to get here.

There are a lot of us elderly folk. We're all different. Most of us have been through several kinds of hell and survived. Don't smile at us as if we're cute. Do not pat our hands or call us dear. We are your elders and possibly your betters. Take a moment. Look into our eyes. We know more than you do. A little respect, please.

Before She Became Invisible

YEARS AGO THERE WAS AN OLD MAN who hung out on the streets of Upper Manhattan. He may still be there, she hopes so. He had a threadbare but distinguished look, and usually had a bottle in a brown paper bag. Every time she passed, he murmured, pretty lady. It seemed to be his calling, his vocation, to bestow compliments under his breath on 110th and Broadway. Upon receiving several expressions of his appreciation she began to feel a responsibility to look good whenever she hit the street. Even just running out for a tube of toothpaste, she checked the mirror. After all, he was providing a service, a couple of words to brighten what might otherwise have been a shabby day, and she didn't want to let him down. Once, as she strode down Broadway to Zabar's, a car full of young men slowed down long enough to yell out the window that she was walking to the exact beat of the music on their car radio. What's not to love about that? Before that, when she was still in her twenties, she was waiting for a bus somewhere in the East Village, on a freezing December night. It must have been two in the morning. A car stopped at the light. The guy riding shotgun rolled his window down and began to hit on her when she heard the driver say, "Don't hassle her, man, it's too cold." She looked inside the car at four men holding what looked like martini glasses and she asked if she could bum a ride to Fifth Avenue and Eighth Street. They obliged. She used to wonder what growing old would be like. What would define her? Would she miss the attention? Now she is old. The city is still there. But she defines herself.

Waiting for Gravitas

I LOOK FORWARD TO MY NEXT BIRTHDAY, because while seventy-nine is getting up there, eighty has gravitas. I could use a little gravitas. Waking up in the morning, it was hit or miss whether I was going to make it to the bathroom in time to pee neatly. I sleep five rooms away and the misses were getting more frequent. God knows where all this pee comes from! I have tried everything, drinking nothing after six o'clock, eliminating salads for supper, and still. Honestly? I don't really care, it's almost thrilling. But what with the mopping up and the laundry I ordered six boxes of Depends from Amazon. They are quite ugly when you first take one out. You'd never guess what it is. It looks like some scaly alien creature that folded itself up and died.

Another accomplishment: I've mastered the art of putting my hair up the way my mother suggested sixty-three years ago. This involves a headband made of somewhat stretchy material. You put it on top of your head like a crown, then spend time tucking all your hair first over and then under it, and you wind up what my grandson Joe called looking "distinguished." It isn't easy, and you have to keep tucking and checking. I keep a mirror on my ottoman hidden under several books and a lot of loose poems. Nobody needs to know the extent of my interest in hair.

The ottoman also holds three face creams, one cane, two dried-up pens, two checkbooks, a bank statement, a beat-up red folder full of old writing, a pair of socks that say BIDEN on them, and a yellow hat with a light you push if there's a blackout. The last two items were birthday presents from my son, Ralph. He drove down from Boston with his little dog Katy, who has one brown and one blue eye. The light on the hat is blinding unless you're the one wearing the hat, but Ralph bought it in case I lose power again. I keep it on the ottoman so I always know where it is. There is also a little packet of unusable black tacks I bought in order to set up a string to stretch across the living room window where two leggy geraniums are reaching for the ceiling, but sag from their own weight. I look forward to a jungle of green leaves and bright red flowers, but have yet to construct the lattice. Something for another day.

On my coffee table is the urn my old pal Chuck gave me. It is the color of a candied apple, the black lid has two birds perched on it. It's lovely. When I opened it, he told me what it was for and that the saleslady had assured him my ashes would fit nicely. I told him of a firm that sells wooden coffins if you want to make friends with death before death arrives. They suggest using it as a coffee table. I have half a mind to buy one. I admit to a shiver now and then if I think of myself reduced to ash. I am comforted by remembering those of my friends who have died. I figure if they can do it, so can I.

Haunted

Snow again today, enough to delay public schools two hours. Dogs woke in the middle of the night when the noisy snowplow went by, lights flashing. I got up just for the hell of it but couldn't find the last two cigarettes I had saved for morning so we all went back to bed. Later, I heard three soft knocks on the bedroom door. Nobody in the house except the dogs and me, and we were already settled under the covers. Last week something was wailing and pounding to get in (or maybe out) through the kitchen door. My dogs barked like crazy and I struggled into my bathrobe. There was nothing in the kitchen, nothing on the porch. Whatever it was had disappeared.

It's pretty clear my house has a ghost. I don't know how it got in or what activated it after twenty years, but something has now begun to make the sound of a door closing when the door is already closed. It has happened twice. Being a ghost seems pretty pointless if you're just messing around with doors. Given a choice, I think I'd prefer to remain dead. Ralph had a friend who lived in an old house with a more interesting haunt. Halfway up the back stairs something grabbed you around the waist. I keep imagining a long line of kids waiting their turns to run up the stairs for the thrill of a ghostly squeeze.

And Then There Is White Noise

THE COOL THING ABOUT WHITE NOISE IS that you hear voices that aren't there. Lots of us experience this. Trust me. We can't distinguish the words, but we hear the inflections of people talking in running water, coffee percolating, air conditioners, ocean waves. There are explanations, having to do with the way the brain tries to make connections out of everything. Think seeing faces in leaves, shapes in clouds. I don't understand the science, although it's reassuring not to be bonkers. I like to think the ghosts of conversations are hanging in the corners of my old house, like cobwebs, and my fan blows them loose.

Inventory

I AM NOT YET A CADAVER nor am I an old woman asleep with her mouth hanging open which is so reminiscent of a cadaver. Crooked tooth in front. Several bottom molars leaning like old pilings on deserted waterfronts. Ate leftover birthday cake for breakfast. Do not describe self as doddering, although fond of the word. Prefer driving rain to sunny days, unless at beach. Notice two big holes in one bedroom curtain. Names of two neurologists to call re: dizzy spells. Cannot drive in dark. Have birthday cake for lunch. Unhealthy desire to set 45 on fire. Love family. Notice three more small holes on curtain, one so tiny as to be cute. Snack on more birthday cake. Still plagued by bouts of worry despite wisdom.

You Know You're Old . . .

WHEN YOU EMAIL A FRIEND about a change in your blood pressure because you know she will be just as interested as you are. When you check your watch to see how long you have to lie in bed until morning. When nothing embarrasses you. When you understand you are breakable by breaking. When you forget what you've forgotten. When at your yearly checkup they ask you to count backward by sevens. One hundred, ninety-three, eighty-six. When you no longer drop everything to answer the phone just because it rings. When you don't wonder what you're missing. When you can't remember the last time you felt guilty. When you stop trying to fix people. When you find the moment roomy enough to live in. When you relish your own company. When you see a young woman with her whole life in front of her, and your first thought is: Thank God that isn't me. Seventy-nine, seventy-two, sixty-five, fifty-eight. But you wish her well.

Diaries

DIARIES WERE HOW I KEPT TRACK OF MYSELF—they were a kind of catchall, anything and everything went in. Messy, of the moment, but they separated one day from the next. And it was a physical experience: dragging the needle-fine point of a pen over the good paper of a Moleskine, feeling the scratch of it, the tiny bit of resistance, this was something I relished. But my right hand is cranky in old age, flat-out refusing to write a legible line, a legible word. What was once a pleasure is now hard work, and the results are discouraging. Does this happen to all of us?

There are a bunch of old diaries floating around, and from time to time I pick one up and flip through the pages. Endless meals and a lot of weather. Something funny Chuck said. Ideas for a story. Bigmom's recipe for fudge. The anything and the everything. If I come across an odd phrase, the scraps of an unfinished thought, I can single it out, see if there's somewhere it wants to go. See if it wants to grow up. Last year I found an assignment buried like treasure in an old diary. Write two pages that begin, "This is a lie I've told before." No clue as to why it had popped into my head, but there it was, smack-dab in the middle of a bygone Thanksgiving dinner. I've been giving it to my students ever since.

Writing things down is not the same thing as writing, but experience put raw on the page kept me sane during a time of trauma. My hand holding the pen, the pen against the paper, here was something familiar I could do, and it calmed me. My diary went with me everywhere, and every tiny thing I felt or heard and hoped and saw, I wrote it down. Eventually I wrote a book about those years, my husband's tragic accident, how our worlds changed. The book, *A Three Dog Life*, would never have been written had it not first been scratched into dozens of diaries. These I keep in the bookcase in my bedroom, but I never open them.

Diaries. I don't like the word "journal." It sounds too formal, almost highfalutin. I especially hate it used now as a verb. Journaling, good God. I imagine people hard at work, perfecting each sentence, every thought, before its time, nothing left underfoot, nothing left to chance. Nothing to unearth years later.

I miss the kinds of things I wrote when my hand still worked, the odds and ends of a uneventful day. Nothing will ever take its place. I'm too old. I lose whole chunks of time to oblivion. Where was Tuesday this week? It never appeared.

A Little Nostalgia from My Red Folder

IT'S A MAN AND A WOMAN and they've climbed to the top of a mountain and it's evening and from where they stand they can see whole worlds and tiny bright cities and since he had coaxed her up this high, because he wanted to show her everything, he had his arms around her tightly because she was afraid of falling. And the sun actually did go down on their right at the exact moment the moon rose on their left, and this would have happened anyway, they both knew that, still they were glad to have seen it together. Whether they lay down and made love or did not make love under a billion stars is of no real interest to anyone, and who they were, and whether he knew the names of every tree and flower and if she loved lavender, or it rained, all these details will vanish like everything else. It happens all the time, you know, the sun goes up and comes down, it rains, we button and unbutton our clothes and turn on our sides to make love because all warm animals need other warm animals right from the beginning, or they go crazy and die. So if he had green eyes and she had blue and if they loved or did not love each other for good reasons or bad, and if they used the old words and did or did not make promises nobody keeps, no matter, let's let it go.

Falling

THERE IS THAT LONG SLOW MOMENT you know you are falling. A split second of curiosity and excitement—what is going to happen? Followed, alas, by landing. One morning ten years ago, I tripped over a shoe, racing for the door to let the dogs out before Daphne peed on the rug again. I hurt my knee and three toes, and lay on my back howling in irritation and surprise and disappointment. I have forgotten millions of important things, but this I remember distinctly. So silly, one foot in the air. Foolish and hurting.

That interminable winter was the first time I'd been afraid of falling. Forget ice and snow. It was possible to catch a toe on my left foot in the pajama cuff of my right foot and almost fall downstairs. It was possible to skid on the kitchen tiles and almost fall. And my old dog, Carolina, was also unsteady on her feet. Cooper is an old dog too, but he never goes upstairs. There were times when Carolina slid down the last few stairs and couldn't get up. When I tried to lift her, she protested, whimpering. I put bath mats under her back feet to give her some purchase, but it seemed a lifetime before she could stand again. So I moved my bedroom from upstairs to the sun porch on the first floor. I ordered venetian blinds for the sun room, which is composed entirely of glass, and an air conditioner that provides both heat and cool. Ralph built me a bed that is low to the ground so Carolina would have no trouble getting on and off. Rain on the glass roof is lovely, and the birds visible, and the trees above my head.

Two Broken Wrists 2015

I WAS EXCITED BY THE NEW GAUZY RED CURTAINS, bored stiff by the dreary stuff that had hung in my living room for years. Getting up on the chair to hang them was easy, getting off was even easier. I fell. It was such a short trip to the floor that I had no time to worry. I heard two tiny distinct snaps as I landed, the sound of wrist bones breaking. It hurt like hell. I laid my hand on a pillow and carried it as carefully as a tray full of brimming martinis. I called Chuck, and he drove me to the emergency room. My cast, the pain, the inability to perform any daily task, were all humbling. I couldn't hold a cup of coffee. Still, it was a brand-new experience, and new experiences were hard to come by. I was seventy-four that year and I was oddly grateful.

But without my right hand, I also couldn't think. Thoughts made a beeline down my right arm to the hand I wrote with, and that was now a dead end. I imagined the inside of my head as an infirmary. My thoughts were pale and thin. They lay in rows of little cots, fingering the bedclothes. Some were coughing. No thought spoke to any other, so I had nothing to write down, even if I could have.

Then, two weeks after my cast came off, my other wrist broke. Chuck and I were waiting in line for a movie, I leaned against a bookstore door, which opened unexpectedly, and I fell. I knew instantly the other wrist was broken. The next morning I called my friend Paul, who drove me for the X-rays, which showed two bones broken, and I received another cast. I'm more fragile than I give myself credit for. I keep forgetting. When I got home, I found a bird in my bedroom—

a bird the size of a tiny teacup, fluttering about. Its presence was almost more alarming than the fact that I'd broken both wrists inside of a month (something I found almost funny). I'd no idea how it got in, but one of my bedroom doors opens on the yard; I got it unlocked and then closed the other door, which leads to the rest of my house. I peeked in after a few minutes and the little thing was standing on the edge of my bed, two feet from freedom. I tiptoed away, made a cup of coffee (which I could now hold), and when I returned, the bird was gone.

I had never felt quite that mortal. But it's a beautiful word, "mortal," rhyming with "portal," which sounds optimistic. And really, who wants to live forever? How tedious life would become. Mortality keeps life interesting. And right now, right this minute, at seventy-nine, that's all I ask.

More Birds

BIRDS HAVE NOW APPEARED IN MY HOUSE on four occasions. Two were of the little fat kind with rosy-brown breasts and stiletto beaks. One cardinal. A bird in your house is supposed to be the harbinger of death, but I gave up on superstition long ago. Knocking on wood, never rocking an empty rocking chair, never stirring with a knife, passing the salt not hand to hand but putting it down first, none of that saved loved ones from harm. I said to hell with that a long time ago. Still, four birds. And a pack a day.

The first was the one sitting on my bed when I got home from the hospital with my second broken wrist. A month later I discovered my hound dog Cooper scrambling after a cardinal flying around the living room! I managed to hang on to my dog and open the door, and the bird flew into the branches of a pine, bright red against the snowy branches.

Late one afternoon, another bird was in my office, sitting on the *Collected Poems of W. H. Auden*. There were no windows I could open, so I went downstairs and hoped for the best. I never saw it again, but I haven't taken Auden out of the bookcase.

But now bird number four is flying around my bedroom! Hopping all over the bed! Again! How this one got in is a greater mystery than how it will get out, although that's still to be determined. I unlock the door, slide it open, and the fourth bird zings out into the wild world.

I will try not to dwell on these visitors, but record it here in case I die, and it turns out I should have paid better attention to these warnings.

Hold on. There is no such thing as "in case" I die.

2016

A FRIEND DIED. Life had dealt her any number of bad hands, but she had emerged a strong, generous, inspiring woman. She was a Catholic, and her faith was unshakable. "She is in the arms of her Savior," I said to myself when I heard the news. I don't believe in heaven or hell. I don't believe in God, but I was as certain of her heaven as that day follows night. Lacking my own, I had faith in her faith.

I told Chuck. "I don't believe in heaven," I said, "but I know she's there." I doubt Chuck believes in heaven, but he is kind. "Heaven was waiting for her," he said. We were lying on separate couches, discussing certainty (death) and mystery (what, if anything, comes next). We decided we were comfortable with mystery. Nothing explained, nothing explained away.

Other Uses for Your Cane

YOU CAN DO A LOT WITH A CANE. It isn't just for balance. You can use its rubber tip to shove a door shut, which is satisfying, especially if you're in a bad mood. You can use its rubber tip to shut off certain wall light switches, which is also satisfying, if you're in a bad mood. Canes are useful for sliding newspapers off an ottoman to the rug when you tire of the news. You can strike the floor for emphasis in an argument. You can use the cane to move things away without moving, i.e., shove the coffee table farther from your chair. You don't need a reason. You can employ the handle to pull something closer without moving, i.e., the coffee table. The tip of the cane can be used to lift fallen clothing and small blankets from the floor. You can use the cane to toss these items onto the sofa, or a different part of the floor, depending on your mood. You can daydream about weaponizing your cane. Walking from one room to another, you can punctuate your progress by striking the floor with varying degrees of force. In a bad mood, you can imagine your cane as a broomstick on which you can fly directly into the Florida estate of the enemy to smear excrement into the occupant's hair and place a tack on the chair where he watches TV.

It Was a Long Winter

I KNOW IT'S ALMOST SPRING BECAUSE there is mud everywhere, tracked in by the dogs. Floors, chairs, couch, bed. I don't mind. At night, varmints abound, and my hound dog Cooper wakes up early, howling. Daphne and Sadie and Carolina start barking, and after five minutes of this, I get up, go into the kitchen, and open the door for the dogs to barrel through. I make coffee.

As soon as it gets light, I sit on the porch. Wind knocks the wet off trees down the block, but doesn't cross to our side of the street. Instead another breeze comes from the north into our yard. How does the wind go about its business? My dog Sadie licks rain off the oniongrass in its black pot and I drink more coffee, light another cigarette. After a bit, I get up from my damp chair, find shoes, walk in the yard.

With spring, the ice is starting to melt. Bits of the past have begun to appear. The top of a carrot, discarded by a dog months ago. Twists of tinfoil, licked clean of whatever they once held. Somebody's shoe. Snow is again in the forecast, but no sign of it so far. Maybe I'll find my daughter's cell phone, my moonstone ring, and the flashlight. There is a book by the wild grass, uncovering itself next to the dripping privet. I bend down. It's *Lawrence of Arabia*, beginning to appear under the drifts of snow.

An Hour Later

IT IS TIME FOR WHATEVER COMES NEXT. When I head inside, a small part of me still thinks I'm going to dive into the day: pay bills, make a few calls, head for the market. Before I have even reached the bedroom door, three of my dogs are already waiting in bed. I sit down (just for a minute), I lie back (just for a minute). Daphne lays her legs over mine, Sadie curls up by my shoulder, and just as I get comfortable, Carolina starts barking, reminding me she needs a boost these days. I get up, lift her next to my pillow, and lie back down. Cooper always sleeps on the living room sofa. He is a dignified dog.

I don't reprimand myself for wasting what's left of my life in bed. It's hard work to be conscious of every moment. Besides, napping is not a waste of time. I am not emptying my head, my mind is filling with words and phrases and half-baked ideas, darting around like schools of fish. This is good for a writer, because even if everything is forgotten when you wake, you know the aquarium is teeming. So then you wait for it to settle so you can see the fish.

Occasionally I fall asleep in the afternoon and wake up in the dark. There is the disturbing question of where am I? What day is it? That is bad enough. Worse, however, is the question what am I? What is this breathing thing I seem to be? This could be a fascinating experience, as if I have been folded into a greater consciousness, but it terrifies me. It rarely happens, thank God, and obviously I figure myself out. It helps to sleep with dogs. They know what I am and they make it clear what it's time for.

Ageism at the DMV

THE UNFRIENDLY YOUNG WOMAN TOLD ME TO READ the bottom line on the chart. "The bottom line?" I asked. "Can't I start at the top?" She shook her head. "Read the bottom line." She didn't crack a smile. "I can't," I said. She asked if I had glasses and I told her they were in the car so she told me to go get them and try again but I'd have to take a new number. I knew the bottom line would be unreadable even with my new glasses, so I skedaddled, lest she decide to confiscate my expiring license. She seemed capable of anything. I went back to the optometrist, who told me it was illegal for her to make me read the last line. "It is happening more and more often," he said, shaking his head. He didn't know why. Was this an example of ageism? he wondered, as he filled out a form that would let me get a new license because I have 20/40 vision in one eye, or something like that, I forget. I carry the slip of paper in my wallet, but have yet to go back to the DMV.

I can't see at night so I only drive in the day, never farther than a mile or two. In this village I can get what I need without going anywhere. I could even go on foot if we had sidewalks. One of these days, if I don't return to the DMV, they will catch me with my dead license. That's the bottom line. I make an appointment with an ophthalmologist.

Oh, good. It turns out that I have cortical cataracts. This explains my blurry vision, the light that messes everything up. I make an appointment for cataract surgery.

There used to be a store in Amagansett called Topping's. It had a lunch counter, groceries, magazines, and comics. Lots of comics. I remember poring over the covers of horror comics, and one image still haunts me. An eyeball, wide open, and a needle descending upon it. Made my hair stand on end, but I kept staring. That's how I imagined cataract surgery. People I knew told me it was nothing, a piece of cake, but all I could think of was watching some sharp instrument as it plunged into my eye.

Instead, I saw lovely dancing blue lights changing hues, punctuated by the occasional bright flash. It was like being at the top of a kaleidoscope, where all the action is. And then it was over. I had an eyepatch on, a bag of medicines to drop into that eye at designated times, and I was good to go. Now, a week later, the sky is a lovely mild shade of blue I'd forgotten existed. If it made a sound, it would be a flute.

Polka-Dot Dress

Curled up on the loveseat on a chilly spring day, seventy-nine years old, I am wearing an undershirt, two sweaters, my purple jacket, warm pajama bottoms, my new cozy socks, and on top of everything, a blanket. I'm also standing on the median at Broadway and 112th, waiting for the light to change. It's the summer of 1978, and a middle-aged woman has just spoken to me in a low voice, saying, "You don't have a stitch on underneath that dress, do you?" It isn't an accusation, she isn't scolding me. She's a coconspirator. I don't remember what I said, but I'm sure I grinned. I remember that dress. It was red with tiny black polka dots, and it buttoned down the front. I bought it at Liberty House, my favorite store, long gone now. Why on earth has this particular memory popped into my head? No idea. But I'm an old woman with too many clothes on, and I'm going to spend a little time remembering that dress, when I wore it, where I took it off. It's a lazy afternoon. I've got nothing better to do.

Memory and Age

ONE OF MEMORY'S ANCESTORS COMES from a root meaning both "to remember" and "to mourn." As if one came attached to the other. To remember is to mourn. That ought to tell us something. But there are gaps in my memory where details should lodge, so much has vanished. My memory is full of holes. Maybe I wasn't paying the right kind of attention to my life. Was I in so great a rush to get to the next thing that I forgot to notice the present? Or maybe the weight of too many memories piled on top of others crushed some, deformed others.

And it's tricky. When I compare what I remember with what my sister Judy remembers, I discover that memory, mine anyway, seems to be an independent creature, inspired by circumstance rather than faithful to it. I could dig my mistakes up by the roots, plant the more literal truth in my damp mind, but inevitably the memory, or the way my brain preserved it, grows back the way it was recorded. I will, for instance, always picture a grape arbor over the rocky pool into which a waterfall fell from a cliff in Sneden's Landing. Judy has told me where the grape arbor actually was (although I've forgotten that again) and patiently pointed out the impossibility of a grape arbor built over a pool. "Think of the grapes falling in," she said reasonably, but I can't help myself. It keeps being there when I remember the place. Not only that, but I seem to have given it marble pillars to hold the thing up. Maybe I was storing some of the things I loved

in one basket, waterfall, ice-cold pool, grape arbor, one thing trig-
gered the others, so I would never forget any of them. When did my
memory do the rewrite? Did I do this behind my own back? How
does this work?

First Impressions Last

MONTHS AFTER MY HUSBAND RICH DIED, a good friend invited me to go away to an island in the Caribbean. I didn't want to go. Another friend, a woman in her nineties, gave me this unforgettable piece of advice: "Always take a cookie when the plate is being passed." I went. I was sitting on the sand one afternoon, and way down the beach at Rum Point, I saw a bird standing on the shoreline, looking out to sea. I thought of my husband and his love of birds, all the yearly lists, the trips he'd taken for the sole purpose of bird-watching, and so I watched this bird. So patient, it never moved.

After a while I got up and walked slowly toward what turned out to be a black plastic bag caught on the end of a stick, but that was simply an interruption, because it is the bird I remember, always and forever the bird, watching the sea, waiting for his true love to return.

What I Just Plain Forgot

LAST WEEK A FRIEND CALLED and in the course of our conversation she brought up a trip we made together, rich with detail, and I had no memory of any of it. And now it is four days later and not only do I not remember what she said, but I've forgotten who she was. All I remember is that I've forgotten the whole thing. When I search my mind for clues it's as if I'm staring at a wall, a smooth white wall. Scary. I make another pot of coffee and light a cigarette. Then I have the brilliant idea of checking my phone to see who called me, and there she is, and very slowly memory collects around me in little drifts. Oddly, I now remember the woman who hosted us, the distant connection I had with her, and how moved I was to meet her. My own separate memory. What is going on?

A few years ago I remember forgetting that two of my grandsons, whom I seldom see, had come for Thanksgiving. How could I have forgotten? When I was reminded, I drew a blank. Even now, all I remember is the never seeing them part. It's like walking through the woods and noticing half the trees are gone. Worse, it's like walking through the woods and not noticing half the trees are gone.

But I can still recite a poem by Philip Larkin called "This Be the Verse," although I had to look up his name, and three poems by Yeats that are found in *The Winding Stair*. I happily remember my mother telling me of the sign on a London street that read, "One flight up for a proper English umbrella." I remember driving down Route 375 with my daughter Catherine who had just gotten her first real pair of glasses and her saying, "I didn't know everything was so pointy."

I forgot that it was a friend of mine who drove my ailing daughter Jennifer to the hospital when she was here for a visit. When Jennifer reminds me, I'm mortified that an act of such kindness slipped my mind, and despair of a recent moment when I could have thanked my friend again. Is it because life is now like a speeding train and everything is a blur? Or is it because life is passing so slowly that I'm mired in the sludge? I do remember now, and what my daughter went through when she was back in Boston, the three days she spent in the hospital there, and how worried I was. It cheers me only slightly that the phrase "slipped my mind" was first recorded in 1340.

My sister Judy is having the same problem. Well, not precisely the same, because her memory for the past is pretty much perfect. On her kitchen counter she keeps an almost empty bag of sugar. She wanted to remember something she has since forgotten, and had tried to tie that important need to the bag of sugar, assuming that every time she saw it, her memory would be jogged. But it hasn't worked. Was it to remember to buy sugar? I asked her, but no, that had nothing to do with it, she tells me.

I remember that I'm out of coffee and must pick it up today before three. I remember (reminded by my daughter) that you water an orchid with an ice cube, but not why. I remember the names of all the dogs I've loved, and where they are buried, but not the years they died. I forget whole decades. I forget what happened when, if I remember what happened at all.

But I know I made chicken soup three days ago and ate the last of it yesterday. I know I had two pieces of toast this morning. I sent an essay to three places two weeks ago but only remember two of them. I know I fed the dogs. I watered the geraniums and my tiny eucalyptus tree. I can still figure out the long-sleeved pullover. As long as I can put it on successfully, I'm good to go. It's when you get your head stuck in the sleeve and keep on pulling, that's when your last marble rolls under the radiator. But still. What happened last week? I come up with nothing. But nothing happened, which is a point in my favor. Does losing memories presage losing my mind? It's odd that I'm not afraid. I'm curious, but I'm not afraid.

Sometimes when I talk to my kids they recount an incident, or a conversation, or an interesting moment in the not-so-distant past and it comes at me completely fresh and new. Every time! I am going to view this as a plus. Nothing is old hat anymore. I don't even wish I could remember what the last thing was.

I figure I have a choice. I can worry myself into the ground. That's one. Or I can think of my failing memory as an achievement. I am finally living in the moment.

Speaking of Forgetting

You know how you find yourself in the kitchen and you can't remember what you're doing there so maybe you put your hands on the cold sink and look out the window but it doesn't help? What works is to go back to the living room, sit down again on the chair you got up from, then retrace your steps back to the kitchen, and somewhere in the hall you remember, Oh! Cheetos! Of course! Then there are the times you get in the car to go somewhere and even before you put the key in the ignition you get this funny physical feeling, a gut feeling, and it means you're forgetting something. It's not anxiety, it's a physical reminder. Amazing! Where does it come from? What part of our body remembers we are forgetting something? Is it the brain cells in our gut? I love it! Maybe you forgot to put water down for the dogs. You left your wallet on the mantel. You didn't bring your passport, checkbook, credit card, birthday present for the party. You can't proceed until it comes back to you, but it almost always does. Is there a word for this? There must be a word for this!

But now how about dying? Dying is no longer a never or even a when, but a how, because maybe you're seventy-nine, like me. What if I get that funny feeling just before I make my final exit? Then what if I have to come back, because if I've forgotten something I'm not done, and I don't want to return, not as a ghost with very little to do, and not as a human. I've been lucky this time around. Tragedy, yes, sorrow and regret and depression, yes. But not being shot in the street. Not starvation. Suppose I'm born into famine? What if my children die in

my arms, their limbs like broomsticks, their bellies swollen? I won't do
human again. If there's such a thing as reincarnation, I hope I have a
choice. I'd rather be a tree, or a bunch of kudzu, or even a moth. I'd
rather be a school of fish. "A whole school?" I can hear my sister Judy
asking. "Why not just one fish?" Because one fish in a school is the same
as the whole school, but different, and I want to know what that feels
like. Plus I love the way they swim in gestures.

Have I Told You This Before?

WE MAKE A RIGHT ONTO 375. Pointing to a scraggly pine on the left that dominates our first sight of the mountain, I'm apt to say, "That's Jennifer's favorite view." Passing the new Sunflower Market, I remark that I still can't find anything, and hate shopping horizontally. When we drive by the midcentury modern shop on Tinker Street, "There is the best stuff in there," I'll say, "and Tony is great. I love him. I bought that crazy lamp from him." I pause, correcting myself: "All those crazy lamps." We drive past the lovely meadow where I often see deer. "Watch out here," I say, "they come out of nowhere!" Then we drive past Sunfrost. "God, how I love their whitefish salad," I say. We pull into my driveway. "That bush was so skinny when it first went in," I say, pointing to the hydrangea tree full of blossoms, "and now it has bark!" and then, "Here come the dogs!"

My passenger is patient until I've said the same thing ten times, then will gently remark, "Mom, you tell me this every time we drive past." I know this, and I can't help myself. I have a theory about those of us who repeat ourselves. We are experiencing something we love over and over again for the first time.

What Her Body Remembers

HER MEMORIES OF BEING YOUNG ARE INFECTED with regret and disappointment, and it seemed her sails were always either luffing or gale-driven. She is happier being old, but her body, which is every bit as old as she is, coming up on eighty, and probably even older when you figure in the cigarettes and alcohol not to mention all the crazy fucking things she did, but that part of her, her housing, as she has come to think of it, is capable of its own memories. The simplicity of desiring and being desired, for example, and in service of that kind of wild, how often she took risks and never ended up dead or even hurt. The chance she is taking now is pathetic by comparison, but it occupies her mind as she drives because she has to think about something, and the fact is that she had to sneak into the car before her dogs realized that was where she was headed. Her dogs who know the minute she reaches for her cane, or puts her shoes on, or does something about her hair, that she is leaving, and would have been through the dog door and waiting by the car before she had even reached the porch. So she had scooped her car keys off the counter leaving everything else behind, except the plant, and gotten out with her dogs none the wiser. Now just the off chance of being stopped by a cop who would find out she had no license with her, and no ID or registration or insurance card (because the dogs would have jumped in to ride shotgun if they'd seen her take her bag, but that's where she had to put the delicate plant she was taking to a friend), and what she would say to the cop about no license and if she should just tell the truth, or maybe burst into tears, as tears were always on hand these days, what with everything and also nothing.

And at moments like this, although there are hardly ever moments like this, she thinks back to that night on East Twelfth Street near Avenue A, when she was with that tall, beautiful Swedish man. She had been helping him carry the mattress they had found in the street on which they would later be banging their brains out if they survived, that is, the crowd of boys that suddenly surrounded them, these silent boys who couldn't have been much more than fourteen years old, whose eyes were dead, and who wouldn't smile, and she remembers the warning from some young men in their twenties maybe, young men standing in a doorway who said don't mess with these kids, we don't even mess with them. And she and the tall, beautiful man were saved by the car on fire across the street, and sirens in the distance coming closer, and the gang of boys melted away. For the first time now she wonders how many of them are still alive.

In those days risks were taken that were actual risks, not just leaving behind her pocketbook and ID and driver's license, God. When she pulls into the driveway safe and sound after delivering the funny plant to a friend, what should come on the radio but the Stones doing "Brown Sugar" and she opens the window all the way, and she turns the volume up as high as it will go, and she cries until the song is over, and when she has cried long enough she goes back up the porch steps, no easy feat without her cane, and there are the dogs as if she's been gone for months and she gives them each a big piece of chicken but doesn't check on anything like messages or email because her body is still remembering the kinds of things her body remembers, she needs to sit down and stay still while she waits for it to forget.

My Old Dog Carolina

MY FOUR DOGS, Sadie, Cooper, Daphne, and Carolina waited by the door. Sadie and Cooper and Daphne shot through, barking their heads off, searching for interlopers. Not Carolina. She took her time. She went into the yard, peed, looked around, and came back inside. Carolina needed a boost onto the sofa, but once there, she was happy. She had a bad stumble late that afternoon. It took me several minutes to help her get to her feet again. I led her into the bedroom, and heaved her up on the bed. Then I went out for dinner with my pal Chuck.

When I got home, I checked on my Carolina. She wasn't in bed. I went through the house calling her name. I even looked upstairs. She was nowhere. This was unlike her, she never went out at night. But even with the car's headlights on, a flashlight, a lot of yelling and wandering through the dark yard, there was still no sign of her. I repeated the search a couple of times, calling and calling. Finally I went to bed, leaving the kitchen door open, hoping to find her there in the morning. It was hard to sleep. The night was supposed to be in the forties, and I worried for her.

I slipped out of the house at first light. Carolina was lying on the grass. She looked beautiful, and at peace, her coat like satin to the touch, but her body was cold and rigid and she was dead. I was shocked and sad and horrified that she had died alone, but there was also a kind of simplicity that impressed me. She chose where she wanted to die, and she lay down under the dark blanket of night.

Carolina was the last of my original pack. My old beagle Harry died, my beautiful Rosie died, and now Carolina. Actually, I suppose I am the last of the original pack. There is way less left of life than the already lived part. I understand now that you can go to bed at night and be dead in the morning.

The house where I live is comfortable, but it is becoming clear that my real dwelling place weighs about 175 pounds. Its hair is turning gray. It smokes and coughs. I feel terrible for this residence whose lease may soon be up. The dogs and I went to bed, all of us subdued. I stare up at the stars, dead for eons, their ancient light still traveling.

Parking Lot Love

SHE IS SITTING IN THE CAR REMEMBERING the parking lot at the end of the road where her grandmother lived. Indian Wells stopped abruptly at the Atlantic Ocean, and at lunchtime there were always working men parked in their pickup trucks eating sandwiches and watching the water. She used to know the names of cars back then. She could tell one from another. She made out in that parking lot with Dicky Ward in his old Packard. She thinks it was a Packard, it was a long time ago.

This was back in the day when Schellinger's Well Drilling was still on Main Street, and his daughter, Judy, was her best friend. There was also Topping's, and the Three Sisters' Tearoom (or was it Two?) and a tiny grocery store with a dime attached to the floor. If you tried to pick it up, it gave you a shock, and the mean old shopkeeper snickered. On hurricane days her family drove to the beach, stared at the insanely huge waves, perfectly safe from wind and water in their car, but struck dumb.

She doesn't like the parking lots at big stores, they remind her of cemeteries. She likes to park at the small local stores in her town. She loves the one at Sunfrost, especially in summer, when her car sits amongst potted plants and trays of flowers. She is part of this community, but she doesn't have to engage. Nobody bothers to look inside a parked car. Once she managed to eat an entire coconut custard pie with her bare hands.

Of course she has choices. She could sit at a table, or by the side of a stream, or on her own front porch. But she likes the parked car. What's that about? she wonders. Is it the comfort of remaining committed to being uncommitted? There she is, having been somewhere, not yet on her way to the next thing. And just for a moment, there is both no next thing, and any number of next things. She could drive home and unpack her groceries, or she could buy a plane ticket to Fiji and never come back. But there she is, sitting in the car. She is in the middle of a pause. She sighs. The pause does not get nearly enough credit.

How We Don't Want to Die

MY FRIEND PAUL AND I AGREE ON WAYS we do not want to die: drowning, burning, being eaten alive. Paul has pointed out that those gazelles don't seem to be suffering when the lion takes them down, so maybe something is either turned off or turned on (state of shock?) in the event you are being devoured, which would be proof of a benevolent universe, something beyond my ken. I want to add I do not want to be murdered. One more thing, I don't want to die with my mouth open. More specifically, I don't want to be found dead with my mouth open. Neither does Paul. He favors dirty martinis and methadone suppositories. Me? I don't know. Maybe sitting in the sun on a nice beach with good waves and blue water and colorful umbrellas and kids in bright bathing suits and my family everywhere, loving where we are, and I could peacefully die on the red beach chair Chuck bought me but maybe this would ruin the beach for my family. I will have to think about it. Paul thinks he might like to die in the hardware store in town. In the housewares department, next to the kitchen towels. I'm still thinking.

PART TWO

STAY-AT-HOME ORDER

*Sometimes we are starving to see
every bit of what is right in front of us.*
— Brian Doyle, *One Long River of Song*

Paper Wasps

ANOTHER RAINY DAY in a long succession of rainy days and I'm bummed that the part of myself that has always kept me company seems to have disappeared. Here we are in the middle of a pandemic, I haven't left the house in ages, and can't write a word. What's the point of being me? I wonder. I'm so stuck. Write about what you notice when you're stuck, I tell my students. Write about what you notice and see what happens. Nothing happens here except bugs.

For instance: I often see one large black ant wandering across the living room floor in early evening. I think there's only one of him. He (I think of it as a he) is always headed toward the dining room but never seems to get there because the next night, and the next, there he is again, walking across the same portion of floor toward the dining room. It's as if he's having his own Groundhog Day. The pale-brown ants, like little freckles, are everywhere and get into everything. One morning they turned up in the jug of maple syrup even though the cap was screwed on tight. My grandsons were horrified and refused to eat their French toast, although I ate mine and part of theirs.

But the most interesting thing is that once or twice a week I find a dead wasp on my bedroom floor. Their presence gets me in gear. Because where are they coming from? The windows haven't been opened in the four years following the discovery of a spider, and wasps are nowhere else in the house. When I find one I use my cane to nudge it behind the bedside table so I don't step on it by mistake. It doesn't occur to me to throw them out. They are too perfect, and too tiny to be rubbish.

It isn't really a bedside table. It's an old filing cabinet, empty of whatever files it once held. The drawers are now full of whatever I don't know what else to do with when I find it in my hand. Uncomfortable earrings, a letter from somebody called William C. Estler to a woman named Mardi, apologizing for taking her to *The Iceman*, which she hated and asked to leave. "I don't like it and I want to go home," he quotes her as saying. Not *The Iceman Cometh* unless he didn't bother with the whole title. Whether it was a play or a movie I'll never know, nor do I know how it ended up in my possession. When I looked him up there were two of him, both dead, one a painter from West Virginia, the other a scientist of sorts in Palo Alto who published an article called "Ion-Scattering Analyzer." There is also a silver bracelet, other scraps of paper on which various grandsons have written darling inauthentic apologies, licenses from four dead dogs I loved, and a necklace I bought because the woman who made it told me the tiny silver sword charm was supposed to cut fear. Why not? I thought.

Today I picked up a wasp by one of its wings and put it carefully in the cap of an old pill bottle from the drawer. The wasp is so completely dead, tiny and beautiful. Its wings are slender, themselves like tiny swords. I'm amazed that I'm not in the least worried by the intrusion. I'm not afraid that I will one day discover dozens of them flying around my bed. What's wrong with me? It seems a natural fear, but I'm just not afraid. Maybe the necklace works whether you're wearing it or not.

They are paper wasps, I looked them up. They chew wood or whatever else is handy and their saliva turns it into paper and they make hanging nests. Somebody had the brilliant idea of giving these wasps colored construction paper, and my God, the nests they made look like beautiful misshapen rainbows. I am kind of in love. Paper wasps are also good for gardens, eating bad bugs. They aren't ornery, like yellowjackets who'd just as soon sting you as not, but they will defend their nests. Well, who wouldn't?

Some time ago I noticed what appeared to be a lightning bug cling-ing (or stuck?) to the side of my sofa, and I've been careful not to dis-turb it. It stayed fixed in place for several days without moving an inch. I wondered if it had decided to die. Then it vanished. Where was it? I wondered. Last night I saw bright blinks amongst the geraniums that climb up my front window. On, off, on, off. There you are, I thought. Oh, good, there you are.

The City, the Sixties

It's 2020. The politics are more than depressing, unless depression can be defined by inexpressible anger. I am full of a disfiguring rage, disfiguring being the first word that occurs to me. It's not the word I'm looking for. What is the word? Something that implies a dead end. I'm old and tired and can't think of a way to be useful.

Turning up in a dream last night was a young man I went out with a lifetime ago. Such different days. I had finally left an unhappy marriage, and was living with my three kids in my parents' place in the city, half a block from Washington Square. It was the late sixties, and I was running all kinds of hot. My poor parents were built-in babysitters. I lied about where I was going, what I was doing. I think they were afraid to ask questions.

"Went out with" is perhaps too formal a phrase to describe our meetings, which often took place on the upper bunk of a tired old double-decker bed in a crowded apartment somewhere in the East Village. We had met at a party where everyone's bag was stolen. Such a flurry of questions followed the robbery: Who? Why? How? And then my bag was returned, dropped off at the front desk of Brentano's, where I worked in the office, keeping a running count of how many copies of which books were sold each day, based on notes from the guys at the register. Everything written on scraps of paper. In those days Brentano's was on the corner of University Place and Eighth Street. Azuma was right next door. Oh, Azuma! Well, missing from my bag was the little bit of money, and added to it was somebody else's bottle of Visine.

There was also a short note signed by the young man who had stolen it, giving me his telephone number, which I immediately called.

I forget his name, he changed it every week to stay incognito. He was one of the leaders of a revolutionary group that seemed to consist of two young black men and a lot of adoring white girls, but I might have made it up about the girls. He was kind and gentle and attentive where my former husband had been curt and cold and abusive, and I was crazy about him. I don't remember what we talked about. I don't even really remember the sex, just that we had a lot of it. At some point he disappeared for a while, ostensibly to go to Canada to learn how to make dynamite. It seemed strange, why Canada? I didn't give a second thought to the dynamite, which never materialized.

I have been trying to remember his face, why we lost track of each other. I wonder if he's still alive. What happened in my dream? His presence has lingered all day. We were so vulnerable. That's what I remember. We were both so vulnerable. And so willing. I remember I had a tiny red address book, and every time he changed his name, I entered the new one, carefully crossing out the one he'd had before. I wish I still had it, I wish I could hold in my hand what I can't put into words.

Oh God, now I am remembering the young man who worked in the stockroom of Brentano's. I liked him very much. He had been dishonorably discharged from the army, after the helicopter he was in was given word that no prisoners were being taken, and the North Vietnamese soldiers they were carrying were to be thrown off while still in the air. This decent young man went nuts.

We slept together once. I didn't know I had the clap until he broke it to me gently, because he had it now, and he had slept with no one but his girlfriend for years. I didn't know where I had gotten it, by then I was sleeping with any man who could fog a mirror, but it wasn't a toilet seat, which is where my friend told his girlfriend he had gotten it. He wrote down the address of a clinic that had just opened, and told me I needed to go. I recall a long walk west, and a room full of sheepish-looking people waiting their turns.

But now dozens of memories are falling like confetti into my consciousness, and my friend Paul has arrived with the makings of fennel salad, and we get to waxing nostalgic about the city we loved, in the days when you could live on a shoestring. That city is long gone, a kinder and more tolerant town, or so I am thinking now. Also vanished are most of our old haunts, even the Riviera closed down, for God's sake. That was the last straw. And although my memory fails me (where exactly was the Ninth Circle?), I'm experiencing a physical rush that my body remembers better than I do, and it's 1969 again.

If I close my eyes I'm back in Washington Square, sitting barefoot on the rim of the fountain with all the other ragtag and bobtails. I'll probably sleep with somebody I meet here today, without even knowing his name. We will wind up in the East Village, or Harlem, or somewhere on West Fourth Street. Trust defined my youth back then, trust and hunger for what I didn't know, and sex felt like a nutrient we released for the planet. The times that were a-changin' have changed, but for a little while I'm going to ignore what went off the rails, and let myself remember what innocence and hope felt like.

Dread

I WOKE UP GASPING in the middle of the night. Out of nowhere. No bad dream, no pain, no nothing. And the thing about waking up gasping is that even when you're wide awake and the original gasps are over, you tend to keep on gasping. It was the first night I'd slept upstairs in years, and I was unprepared for the silence of the downstairs, of how big and how uninhabited and how right underneath me this emptiness was. I was terrified of the gasping, terrified of the downstairs. I was also terrified that I was terrified, which is the double whammy. It would have helped if I could have given it a name. "Death" might have done the trick, but death didn't ring a bell. I spent the rest of the night downstairs by the radio in order to hear human voices, because I'd lost all sense of myself as any particular kind of being. I might as well have been a lizard in a nightgown, hunched over in my chair.

Whatever it was, wherever it came from, it's still around. It comes and goes. I feel it in my body, like a shadow, darkening everything I see and think and feel. If I can figure it out, "out" being the operative word, maybe I can dispel it and move on.

The Only Other Time

FIFTY YEARS AGO SHE BURIED what she didn't want to know with the anger she didn't want to feel, so when it came back for her, as it always does, it had no name. She remembers long-ago mornings when that house was empty, her kids at school, her husband at work, clutching the arms of the chair thinking, Maybe it's all that dark woodwork, which was ludicrous and pathetic, and she feels such pity for that girl, a stranger to her now. When the failing marriage ended, the dread was gone. An old woman, she has long since learned to put two and two together. Dread? It's a red-hot screaming message that something has to change. But here she is again, clutching the arms of another chair, without a clue. Because now? At her age? Come on.

Damn It

JUST WALKING ALONG FEEDING THE DOGS or emptying the dryer and out of nowhere dread shows up, like a shadow moving in her gut, and everything comes to a standstill. Sometimes it comes and goes, like when clouds scudding across the sky suddenly blot out the sun. Like an eclipse.

2020 Reminds Me of That Partial Eclipse

"DO NOT LOOK DIRECTLY AT THE SUN" is what we've been cautioned for weeks. My daughter Jen and her twins are making the viewing apparatus out of an empty Cheerios box, tinfoil, a pinprick, a cut-out square near the bottom to look through, and they are now carefully lining the inside with white paper. I watch for a while, then move to the back porch where the crows are doing their call and response. Ralphie, age twelve, joins me. This is three years ago, no, four. I am cawing. "I'm a good cawer," I tell him. "CAW!" but there is no answer. I caw again: "CAW CAW CAW!" No answer but silence.

"Maybe you're saying the wrong thing," Ralphie suggests.

"What do you mean?" I ask.

"Well, maybe they're asking, 'Where are you?' and you're saying, 'I like olives.'"

The viewing box is finished, and we hit the beach. We love Head of the Meadow despite the dune we have to traipse over, as difficult to go down as it is to go up. At precisely one-thirty, I'm told the sun is visible inside the box, a small circle of light with a sliver of shadow encroaching on one side. I can't see it, no matter which way I adjust the angle, but to tell the truth, I don't want to watch an eclipse taking place inside a cereal box. I give up and return to my chair, head back, face to the sun. A few people walking by see what the kids are doing and stop, and Jen offers them a turn. They take the box as if handling something radioactive, and moments later, "Oh my God, I see it, I see it," they cry, and after many a thank-you, they continue their stroll to the water.

If this were a total eclipse there would be something to watch, but not on the East Coast, not on Head of the Meadow beach, not here. The light is growing dimmer. Very slowly the hot day cools around me. Strange.

Millions of small silver fish glint all over the sand, shining like tiny twists of tinfoil. At the water's edge, a small girl is bending, scooping, straightening up, and throwing handfuls of the dying fish back into the waves. "If their tails are wagging, they're alive," she cries, bending over again. She is joined by a bunch of other kids, but the job is endless and futile.

A woman walks over to us. The eclipse has upset her. The dead fish have upset her. She has read a book recently about the end of everything. She has been prepared for the whole beach, the dunes, the parking lot, everything, to collapse beneath her feet, and the sea to rush in and cover us all. She still seems nervous. "It's over," we tell her, because it is, "and we're all still here." The tiny fish are being chased by mackerel, we tell her, and they are heading in the wrong direction, the beach, maybe the only direction left to them. An elderly man says that in all his thirty-five years here, he has never seen the like. The woman lingers, then wanders away, still apprehensive. I want to read the book but have already forgotten the title. Her fear was primitive and powerful, and despite myself, I stare at the horizon, waiting, ready to grab my family and run.

She Ate an Orange

MY CAR SITS IN THE DRIVEWAY, gathering dust. The battery is dead again, or something. My sister Judy says it might be the alternator, whatever that is. She starts to explain but I'm only pretending to listen. I don't care. The virus is everywhere. Jennifer made a big batch of her famous soups and sauces and put them in mason jars and found someone to drive it all from Boston to me in Woodstock, along with olives and pasta and rice and garbanzo beans and chocolate chips and an ice cream maker. I'm set. All this and Paul, too. I make a list on Monday and Paul buys my groceries on Tuesday.

Besides, I stopped driving farther than a mile shortly after my car flipped over on Tinker Street a couple of years ago. Chuck had missed the early bus, and called asking for a ride into Kingston. I was driving into the blinding early morning sun, and when my car scraped against an invisible parked car, I yanked the steering wheel to the left. A second later, with a shockingly loud crash, I was hanging upside down in my seat belt. Once I could make sense of my new surroundings, noticing the ceiling below and the floor above, my only clear thought was, Oh, good, the car isn't on fire, and then, having hollered "HELP!" to no effect, I leaned on the horn and waited for Woodstock to wake up. I don't know how long it was before a bunch of men appeared, seemingly out of nowhere. One of them managed to get into the back seat, reach over, and undo my seat belt, and another pulled me through I-don't-know-what opening. My memory of these logistics is blurry. They spoke little English, and I thanked them over and over in Spanish. They smiled and nodded. I hope I hugged them all. When we heard sirens, these saviors melted away. I was unhurt, turned down a trip to the hospital, and a cop drove me home. The car was a total wreck. It occurs to me to wonder why I didn't panic, but there's a lot to be said for being in shock. The men who rescued me were probably in danger of being deported, and I had a wild desire to set the entire Trump administration on fire.

My favorite memory of the overturned car didn't even happen. Chuck, when asked what I did while trapped inside the car, replied, "She ate an orange." It wasn't true, but I love that he thought me capable of such nonchalance.

What I Miss

HERE'S WHAT I MISS. Nothing deep, nothing to write home about, just the ordinary act of grabbing a coffee at Bread Alone, exchanging pleasantries with the manager, brushing up against other people, saying sorry or excuse me or not, nodding hello to people I know, or sort of know. I miss finding an empty table where I can sit down with my coffee and my notebook and pretend to write, when I'm really just eavesdropping, or looking around. I miss going into Birchtree, or Woodstock Design, and picking out a shirt big enough that I don't have to try it on, staring at the earrings in a glass case, almost buying a hat, picking up a couple of pairs of ridiculous socks. I miss walking down Tinker Street, stopping at the Golden Notebook, sitting on the chair they provide next to their poetry section, looking through one skinny book of poems after another. I miss having lunch at Shindig with Chuck and grinning at the waitress who knows exactly what we will both order. It's not deep conversations I miss, I don't do deep conversations, it's the friendly nods exchanged with people I have seen day after day, year after year. All the ordinary stuff that enriched my life.

But You Never Know

I LOOK AT MY WATCH AND AM APPALLED TO SEE it is only ten-thirty in the morning. My God, what will I do with the rest of this day? Earlier I saw four blue jays on the grass together. Normally, this would be something to savor, but the moment passed and the birds flew away. Now I'm watching my dog Daphne gobble up some carrots I'd left for the squirrels, carrots she would have ignored if I'd offered her one inside. There must be something festive about coming on a carrot unaware.

Wait. That is ringing some kind of bell.

Something something something unaware. What is this reminding me of?

It takes a few minutes to remember entertaining angels unaware. Hebrews 13:2: "Be not forgetful to entertain strangers: for thereby some have entertained angels unawares." I am now roused from my stupor. Then my phone rings; it is my friend Adele. Adele asks me hard questions and I am obliged to seek answers. Four blue jays, one black dog, and Adele. Six angels and it isn't even noon. I'd better keep my eyes open. And now here comes my grandson Joe, with a lattice he bought for my window, and his toolbox. He is wearing a mask. An hour later, and the geraniums are woven through the lattice, two flowers starting on one of the plants.

I must remember you never know, you never know, you never know.

Night

AN OLD FRIEND OF MINE IS AFRAID OF THE NIGHT SKY. I thought she was kidding, but she wasn't. She won't talk about it, if I so much as mention the stars or, God forbid, the moon, she threatens to hang up the phone. I am left wondering why. So much space, empty and everywhere? Too much, just too much empty? Except for the lonely moon and all those dead stars? I don't know. My dread has nothing to do with the night sky. I wish that was my problem, it is so specific.

Casadastraphobia, the fear of falling into the stars. Everything has a name.

Minor Worry

I HAVE A CROOKED FRONT TOOTH (my left central incisor, I looked up its name) and it has a small but pushy neighbor, nudging it forward. Nature abhors a vacuum, and as this continues, the crooked tooth may wind up sticking straight out of my mouth. Like a street sign. That's one hideous possibility. The other is that whatever shifty moves my little tooth is making may result in the big tooth with its back to the world, having nowhere else to turn. Talk about the dark side of the moon. I heard this all from a dentist sixty-five years ago, everything that might eventually become of my mouth if I didn't get braces, but I was fourteen, I had no receptors for "eventually," and I didn't want braces. Besides, the tooth was barely out of place back in 1955. Eventually is finally here, but so is 2020. My tooth is just a distraction.

Cluster Flies

I AM GOING OUT OF MY MIND, writing nothing, noticing nothing, beginning to wonder where the hell this word "boredom" came from, because sometimes the DNA of a word answers a question you didn't know to ask. I remember once looking up the word "acceptance," because I was having a hard time with something I couldn't change, and among the words that acceptance evolved from was one that meant "a thread used in weaving." And at once I understood. Maybe it frays, maybe it breaks, but you have to weave it in and keep on weaving. But, damn it, boredom seems to have no traceable origin. Somehow, out of a word that means to drill, and/or the hole that is drilled, appeared this listlessness, this utter lack of curiosity, tinged, at least for me, with irritation. And this meaning showed up seemingly out of nowhere, it has no antecedents. Boredom arrived in our vocabulary, fully formed, in 1852. Something to do with the publication of *Bleak House*, but I can't follow the connection. No culture wants to claim it, boredom is an orphan.

Somewhere once I read, or think I read, that when a boxer is on the ropes, fending off blows from another boxer, this is called being bored. I love this, being a fan of understatement. Trouble is, I can't find the source, and "I'm so bored" suggests something unexamined, something internal. A self-inflicted wound. It's probably the precursor to depression. I need to pay attention.

So here I sit, drinking my coffee; one minute I'm gazing into nothing in particular, the next I'm staring at the window, where dozens of flies have suddenly morphed out of thin air. Spontaneously combusted! They can only be cluster flies, my least favorite kind. Hunting under the sink for something, anything, to do them in, I grab a bottle of Windex, hoping it will finish them off. They are single-minded, these flies, they stick together and they never leave the window, their sole purpose seems to be to bump toward the light, the warmth, the window, and I start spraying. The flies struggle, but I persevere, and after what seems like forever, wings held tight against their bodies, the flies are sliding down the glass on streams of the liquid, like a fatal carnival ride. I tell myself this has to have been a better death than the flyswatter. I get the Dustbuster and vacuum them up. Ugh. I don't know how to open the Dustbuster, which is ridiculous, and the flies are still in there, one or two beginning to stir. I put it on the porch. I'll wait until Catherine comes over, she's good at things like this. I sit back down in my chair. The dogs have slept through the whole ordeal, still asleep on the couch. I don't think dogs are ever really bored.

As luck would have it, right outside my window I notice a feather, caught perhaps on a loose strand of spiderweb, floating back and forth, round and round on a breeze that keeps changing its mind. Where did it come from? The original word in English has always meant "feather," but its plural means "wing." Loving this, I am still watching as this small white anonymous feather that I might easily have missed drifts into, then out of my life.

Cooper

MY DOG COOPER DIED. He had been shaky for weeks, needing help up and down the porch steps, a boost onto the sofa. He had lost any interest in food. He still went out every morning, and I'd watch him wandering in the increasingly green grass, poking around after whatever varmints had had the temerity to cross our nighttime yard. He wasn't howling anymore, he wasn't even barking, and being a bluetick coonhound, Cooper's howls had been the stuff of legend. Instead, after a slow careful examination of his domain, he looked around for a quiet place to sleep. I would find him on the softening pachysandra under a viburnum bush, or in a thicket at the end of the yard, and when the forsythia turned itself into a green and yellow tsunami, there he was sleeping peacefully under its shelter. Cooper wasn't in pain, his last checkup had warned of nothing dire on the horizon, but he was showing all the signs of an old dog, getting ready to die an old dog's death. I wanted to respect that. But his last hours were hard, when he could no longer rise, when he lost control of his bowels, this dignified dog was bewildered and in distress, and there was blood in his stool. I was horrified. Sitting next to him on the floor, I tried to comfort him, but it was terrible to witness. I hate euphemisms for death, but just as my friend Dawn found someone to help him let go, just as she was giving out my address, I looked down at Cooper, and at that moment he died. He slipped away on his own, just as quietly as if he had tiptoed out of the room.

I was left wishing I had taken better care of him. How could I have been so certain the natural process would spare him suffering? Why had I not had a plan B?

I keep thinking I see him. Sometimes I hear him walking around. My dog Daphne has taken over his role as our early warning system. Instead of in bed with me and Sadie, Daphne now sleeps where Cooper always slept, in the living room on the loveseat. A howl at one in the morning used to alert us to the possibility of a bear, or a raccoon, or who knew what prowling too close to the house. Now it's Daphne barking. I am still haunted by guilt. I should have been able to spare him those final hard hours. But guilt and grief are for the survivors. I keep reminding myself that Cooper was a wonderful dog. He lived a good dog's life and then he died.

I don't know what Cooper knew, but if I were to describe his behavior in those last weeks, I would say he was composing himself. I want to compose myself, as Cooper did. I don't believe Cooper was afraid of dying, he was innocent of that awareness. I'm more bothered by the idea of fearing death than I am afraid of dying. This is perhaps too fine a distinction, but today it's working for me.

Anxiety

SHE CAN TALK HERSELF INTO AND OUT OF ANXIETY. She has had a lot of practice, after all. She has four kids, twelve grandchildren, one great-grandchild, and there is always someone or something to worry about. And, oh God, she knows how heartbreaking life can be. She is quite capable of inventing worries when there are none. That ghastly episode with the head lice thirty years ago comes in handy; she has been imagining infestations ever since. When all is going well, and she allows herself to relax, anxiety appears again, like a correction. She is learning to have faith that her family will get through whatever comes their way, but she has to learn it over and over. Dread is the showstopper. She can't talk her way out of that.

Come night she watches movies with zombies in them. She finds them a refreshing change from the real horror, which is the news. After countless hours, she is beginning to believe that zombies will arrive at some point. They are probably already here. It is too bad that even death doesn't set them free, because they come back as zombies again no matter what and are doomed to stumble around in filthy clothes with their mouths hanging open and no lips so their teeth and gums show until someone chops off their heads or sticks something sharp through one of their eyes.

Horrible, but happily not her problem.

An Unexpected Fix

DREAD KEEPS TURNING UP like a long-lost cousin, a real pain in the ass, but family. Sometimes it accompanies my days, but always shows up at night. I watch the sun slide down the far wall, and it begins to build. Dive into it, I've been told. Discover the reason, and it will vanish. One night, lost in fear, I decide this unwelcome visitor must have a face, and the only one here is mine, so I look in the mirror for clues. My God, I look just like my mother! What is this haughty expression doing with my features? I am trying to make sense of this, trying to parse what haughty has to do with fear, or fear with haughty, and I am suddenly distracted, ready to reassess my mother and her moods. Did her haughty look mask what my mother sometimes called "a feeling of impending doom"? My poor mother, forgive me, I didn't know. Curiosity dispels the dread for a millisecond, but then it returns. Luckily, right next to me on the loveseat my old dog Daphne begins to fart. I pull my scarf over my nose. The farting continues. Ah, the competition between existential dread and a farting dog, how very amusing! The farts are winning this battle. I'm starting to feel better. It must be the slices of leftover ham I gave her this afternoon. Tomorrow? Ask Paul to buy more ham.

Despite Everything

IN SPITE OF ALL THAT MIGHT BE SAID, and despite what I have to say about all that might be said, today is sunny, and it's the sixteenth of May, the first day I don't need a sweater, and I'm sitting on the porch just sinking into spring. If I had a shred of ambition, I'd try to write a poem, because I'm watching the ingredients of a haiku taking place right there in my yard. My magnolia bloomed this year with such an extravagant display of pink and white that for weeks she has been practically afloat, putting words like "wedding" into my mouth, and "bride," and I can't help staring because the wind, the errant wind is right this minute undressing my magnolia, hundreds of loosening blossoms fall to the ground, and here come the adjectives, one after another: "unruly," "careless," "impertinent'; but I don't think she minds, she was probably getting ready to do it herself; forget the haiku, there are far too many syllables ("luscious," "deshabille," "honeymoon") and here I am, left with only a title, *in flagrante delicto*. Caught in the act.

Memorial Day Weekend

POURING RAIN TODAY. It's the start of the Memorial Day weekend. Last year I joined Zena Rec, a bright blue swimming pool in the woods, always full of kids in the water, parents on the patio sunning their winter bodies. Last summer Catherine's boys learned to dive, joyously screaming. They are often admonished for running, but running is their mode of travel. These kids have never, as far back as I remember, walked. Last year Jennifer and her twins were on their way down from Boston. It was a rainy day, and the trampoline was slippery. Cooper was still alive and he would be coming back from the yard, licking the rain off his feet, rolling on the red sofa, moving to the blue sofa, back to the red sofa, as was his wont. I am sitting in my chair, wide and soft, reminding myself of my grandmother, whose own chair was wide and soft. Her radio sat on the table tuned to the Brooklyn Dodgers. She loved a glass of cold beer. "I just want to freeze my throat," she once whispered. I look at my watch. It is five-thirty. Where is everyone? Silly question. It's 2020. Nobody is coming this year.

A New Solution for Dread

THERE'S A FIRST-CLASS STAMP AFFIXED to the floor of my porch. It wasn't there before. The first thought in my untethered mind is that if my house is trying to mail itself somewhere, it isn't going to get very far. Where was it planning to go? The beach? Then, my mood being what it is these days, my mind goes straight to hurricanes, and global warming, all manner of devastation. I haven't left this house for nine weeks because of the coronavirus and I'm probably more than a little nuts. I leave the stamp where it is, a perfect example of insufficient postage and ridiculous hope. It's only a stamp, but it makes me smile, and these days, I take what I can get.

I'm thinking about the beach. My grandmother lived on a road in Amagansett that stopped at the Atlantic Ocean. Growing up, we were there every summer, and in good weather, we spent most of our time in the water. On hurricane days, when everyone else had gone back to the city, my family drove to the beach, sat in the car rocked by wind, and watched the ocean tear itself apart. That's when I first felt the kind of awe that makes you tremble. The kind of awe that's close to fear.

I want to write about fear, the kind that has no face, no edges, no logic. Free-floating fear has plagued me for months. It began when I woke out of that sound sleep gasping for breath. I'm afraid of the rooms in my house, afraid of the fading sun, afraid of my bed. I've tried meditation and guided meditation and gratitude and music and finding my happy place but nothing has worked. Flattened by panic one night last week, I had a crazy inspiration. What if I make up a story that would justify this kind of fear? For me it always comes back to the ocean. So there I am, lying in the fetal position on the sofa, my dog Sadie with her head on my ankles, and I start to imagine myself on the beach after a hurricane, and something ragged is chasing me, and the sand is too soft to run fast and it is getting dark, and the whatever-it-is is gaining on me so the only safe place to run now is right into the ocean, the dark wild ocean, and I thrash through the broken surf so I can dive the first huge olive-green wave before it breaks on top of me, then there's another to dive, and another, the breakers stretch to the horizon and I am gasping again because the undertow is pulling me down and I'm going to drown until some crazy riptide drags me farther out to sea, turns sideways toward Montauk but taking me farther and farther from shore and my panic is turning into the psychic equivalent of a soundtrack, matching the story I am telling myself—and the next thing I know it is daylight and I am waking up on the sofa, home and dry.

I offer this simple solution to anyone suffering from nameless fear: write yourself into a story where you stand half a chance of surviving, and do, at least until morning.

A Lot of Nothing

THESE DAYS I DO A LOT OF NOTHING. I'm good at doing nothing, but when I'm done doing nothing, I don't know what to do. We're in the middle of a pandemic. There's nowhere to go. I haven't driven my car in months. I should pay my taxes, call the septic guy, write some letters, pay my bills, but I am paralyzed. Let's see. Today. It's five-fifteen in the morning. What do I do? I pull a few hairs out of my head and hold them up to the light to make sure I don't have head lice. Sometimes the follicles look like nits, so I use a magnifying glass for closer examination. One of my younger grandsons has head lice, and my head is itching. Seven hairs, no lice. It's almost disappointing so I pull out another bunch of hair. Still no lice. My interest wanes. Then I pick up a catalogue and look at mattress pads. For years I've longed for the fleece ones that they say are washable but I don't believe it, and I don't need a new mattress pad. Then I look at feather beds which I also don't need, although they look inviting. I drop the catalogue back on the floor. I'm depressed, but not that depressed. There's still enough of me around to like my hair better today than yesterday, and where there's a shred of vanity, irony is not far off. That might cheer me up. I sit in my chair while my foot imagines a gas pedal on the rug that I can floor to get to the day when everything changes.

Maybe I Should Paint Again

TEN YEARS AGO I WAS NOT DEPRESSED, I was obsessed. It was a little odd, and I can't explain it, but all I wanted to do, and all I did, was make paintings of fried eggs, sunny-side up. I made individual egg portraits, group egg portraits, paintings of eggs snuggling together, families of eggs placed side by side, eggs dressed as ghosts for Halloween. I painted on glass with oil-based house paint that came in quarts. Despite all the other colors, it was yellow that called to me. Dipping a stick into the thick oily paint, then holding it steady above the glass, I could produce a perfect circle, drop by drop. It was magic. When the yolk was firm, I added the white. I could never have done it on purpose—some things only come about by accident—but in one particular painting, two little eggs wound up with strings attached. Somehow I had produced two small fried eggs on pogo sticks. I was so proud. I felt a little like their mother.

Interview

A SCHOLARLY BOOK ABOUT WRITING has just been published and it includes one of her tiny essays, and the editors are going to interview her about the way she wrote it. She is nervous. She tried to prepare, but it is hopeless from the git-go. She can't explain why she writes the way she writes. If she'd stayed in college she would have the right words. The concepts. But she left halfway through freshman year and never went back. Take this piece she's writing now. Why is it in third person? She is sitting right there in her chair, it's her fingers on the keyboard, why doesn't she say so? Well, sometimes she needs to see herself in the distance, the past, for example, or the future, or in a sorry mood. And sometimes when the first person can't think straight, the third person steps in. Also, she gets tired of herself, all that me me me. The third person is always handy, always willing. And it knows more than she does.

She is asked why she wrote a sixty-one-word sentence with so many ands instead of commas. She has no clue except to say it was a long trek to the top of the mountain and there was no stopping to rest because there were no resting places and therefore there were no commas. Wait, there were two. Right? Real life is full of commas, of course, but when both the sun and the moon and a mountain are involved, well, punctuation falls short, don't you agree? Next she finds herself avoiding the question as to why don't they have names? because the answer to why don't they have names is so obvious that she doesn't want to appear rude, but "he" and "she" are sufficient and who would be so specific, so confining, as to induce claustrophobia. As it is they are already crammed into five sentences along with the entire evening sky not to mention the tiny bright city visible in the distance below and a few thoughts about love and the weather. On top of that, names might distract from what is and what is not happening, burdening the reader with who is this Robert, who is this Joan? Because names come with different tails, right? Like dogs? And finally the interviewer wonders about her thoughts on calling attention to the idea of truth in an essay, but she doesn't understand the question and consequently the only part of her brain still functioning is the back of her mind, and that door locks from the inside, meaning she can't get in until it wants to get out. There is a terrible pause, which could be represented not by commas, but rather a parenthesis (in which she is held captive and rendered speechless), during which the kind interviewers pick up the ball and answer their own question, and the session ends with her words of thanks, profuse and heartfelt, exclamation points sticking into everything.

Spider

A LARGE BLACK SPIDER RODE INTO THE HOUSE yesterday with me and the mail. It was hidden between some bills, a small package, and a flyer advertising window replacements. I was sitting in my chair, sorting through everything, and suddenly there it was, the size of a fifty-cent piece, sitting on an envelope. I emitted a little shriek and shook it to the floor where it instantly vanished. I imagined it under the sofa, getting ready to spin its web and collect whatever came its way so it wouldn't come mine. As long as I couldn't see it, I was fine. Then this morning, as I looked through the *New York Times Book Review* at all the books I was never going to read, there it was again, the spider, sitting right next to me. As if we knew each other! As if we were friends! I sprang out of my chair and it disappeared under the cushion. I didn't really spring out of my chair. I rose creakily and staggered across the room with my cane. I don't think it touched me, but I don't think you can feel a spider touching you, they are so light. It would be like something happening in a dream. Age has lessened my fear of spiders, I am willing to coexist as long as I can't see them. As long as they aren't sitting right next to me. As long as they're not in the room where I sleep.

Now I must digress, going back sixty-three years to a summer my family spent in Cambridge, England, where the spiders are on steroids. I think it has something to do with the damp. One night, as I was trying to fall asleep, something landed with a soft but audible pat next to my head. I turned on the light, and there, the size of a salad plate, was a spider. I screamed, my father came, and we watched as the thing disappeared behind the bureau. My sister Judy slept in another room, her bed the size of a cot, but for the next two months I slept with her. For the last sixty-three years I have slept with a pillow over my head, just in case.

I figure I have two options. I can abandon my favorite chair, and the view out my window, or I can find my Dustbuster and lift the cushion. For the time being, I have chosen the former, it can have the chair. I've eaten two ham and cheese sandwiches in a row because being displaced made me hungry. I don't like the other chair I'm sitting in. It isn't big enough for Sadie to jump up and drape herself across the back, providing me with a shawl made of warm dog.

By midafternoon, I give up. I find the Dustbuster and lift the seat cushion off my chair. No spider. I vacuum the seams anyway, replace the cushion, and resume my vigil by the window. Life is restored to its familiar pattern. My spider has found a better place to hide. Oh, good. Now it can do its work and I can do mine. There is a squirrel manhandling one of the plums I set out. I watch as it disappears with the fruit into the hydrangea tree, the branches and blossoms shake like crazy, and then the squirrel descends without the plum. It is getting on for fall.

Three days later my friend Eva announces that there is a big spider in my shower. I get up and take a look. I think it's the same one. It can't climb the slippery slope of the shower wall, although it keeps trying. I don't want to kill it, but I don't want it in my shower either. What if it walked across one of my feet? Catherine is here, and she is an old hand at this. She traps the spider under a glass, slides a postcard underneath, and releases it outside. Catherine isn't afraid of anything. She has a pet corn snake that she wears around her neck like jewelry. It is five feet long. The shed skins (which she keeps draped over doors) look dry and fragile as if they would fall to pieces if you so much as looked at them, let alone touched. She also has two cats, and used to have some sort of iguana-type creature, or maybe it was a horned toad, but it had to be re-homed because nobody liked to hold it and it grew wild. It bit everybody while they were trying to feed it. In exchange, she was given three rats of different colors that came with names she has changed.

Catherine tells me there is another spider in my bedroom, next to a wicker basket of knitting. I gave up knitting several years ago, but still have quite a lot of wool. It seems a fitting place for a spider to live. Catherine, who is fond of reminding me that wherever you are, you are always within eight inches of a spider, reminds me again. I eyeball the distance between basket and bed. It's a good ten feet. What the hell. God knows I've gone to bed with worse. I can sleep with a spider.

No Attention Span

SHE CAN'T READ THESE DAYS. Poems, maybe, if she's lucky and if they're short. But prose? Her attention dissolves after a sentence, sometimes half a sentence. She looks down at the rest of the page and her heart sinks. So many words! She tried to reread Lawrence Durrell's *Prospero's Cell*, but couldn't get past the first sentence. Fortunately, the first sentence is so good there was no need to read further:

"Somewhere between Calabria and Corfu the blue really begins."
Can't beat that.

From My Chair by the Window

SITTING BY THE OPEN WINDOW ON A LOVELY DAY is almost like sitting outside. Better. It's where I spend my daylight hours. I have a view of a bare patch of earth under a huge hydrangea tree where I place bits of fruit and flakes of dried oatmeal mixed with nuts and watch whatever small creatures come by. Chipmunks, birds, squirrels, rabbits. There is a lot of taking turns, no squabbles. I never sit outside in one of my nice orange chairs, enjoying a bit of a breeze, looking around at the trees and wild grasses and geraniums and flowers whose names I forget but they are a deep red. Begonias. Outside is too big, too astonishing. It is like trying to curl up in a cathedral. Inside is comfort, the paintings on my walls, my books, small things I love that stay put. There is the loveseat where I nap with my dogs. We're not escaping reality. We're surviving the day.

Blocked by Facebook Due to a Password Glitch

FACEBOOK DOESN'T KNOW WHO I AM TODAY. It asks me if I know me, and if not, would I like to be my friend? It seems an innocent question, and it's posed by computer code, but it comes with an undertow that drags me into deep water. Would I want to be my friend? I don't think so. Not that I wouldn't like me and trust me, but I am lazy and jealous of my solitude and that might present a problem. I might not want to meet for coffee with myself and I wouldn't show up at my parties. I might not recognize me if we passed on the street. I might call myself up during the wee hours with some problem I am struggling with, and grumpily hang up, causing a rift between us. What then?

Who will I talk to if I can't stand myself?

Summer Day

THE DOGS ARE BOTH ASLEEP. My telephone hasn't rung in two days. There is a lone fly drifting aimlessly around the room, spending most of its time banging itself against the window. There is nothing I can think of to recommend a fly. There can't be much nutrition there, and its wings are nothing special, except to the fly. Viewed under a microscope might reveal more, so I Google "fly wings under a microscope" and find barbs on the edges and hairs all over. The only thing I admire is the simplicity of its name: fly.

There is a pile of clean laundry on the sofa where it has lain untouched all week. Maybe learning how to fold a fitted sheet will rouse me from this stupor, teach me something useful. Paying close attention to the Google video, I try to neatly pack one fitted corner into the opposite fitted corner, but there is such a commotion of wrinkles and ridges, it's like trying to stuff one ear into another, and I give up. The sheet returns to the pile. Next I switch on the radio and catch the tail end of a conversation about slugs. I am late to this party, but it seems scientists can teach something to one slug, don't ask me how, or what, then feed its RNA to another slug who suddenly knows what the first slug learned. This is very interesting. Next the speaker makes mention of a slug who learned something I can't quite catch, it all goes by so fast, then it died and part of it was fed to another slug who learned what it was the dead slug had learned, and all I want to know is if the second slug can now remember dying or, even better, being dead? This sends me straight to Googling Yeats's "Leda and the Swan" because of the line "Did she put on his knowledge with his power," although it has no bearing on slugs. Still, it's a plus, because, well, Yeats, and because the days are slow and so uneventful that the only news is that I'm falling in love with three dying hydrangea blossoms. I picked them ten days ago before the deer could eat them. I put them in a small vase because they were small, filled it with water and set them on the counter. Their slender stems were frail, too frail to support even these small blue blossoms, and they collapsed over the rim of the vase, like a newborn slumped on a mother's shoulder. I can't bring myself to toss them out. They aren't garbage.

Bears can't get in my garbage cans anymore, since my daughter did something tricky with a dog leash I can't explain, although a neighbor thought it was my garbage bears had spread in his woods and left me a cranky message suggesting I spray my cans with ammonia. I took my trusty cane and waded through his woods to prove it was not my garbage, I don't eat chicken tenders, do not have small children who wear diapers, and do not live at number sixteen. I am number eleven. I called my neighbor back to explain this and tell him whose mail I found there and have completely forgotten his response.

I repotted a tiny eucalyptus tree my daughter gave me and placed the pot on the windowsill next to my chair where it gets a lot of light. According to Google the five-inch tree needs full sun and nitrogen, and I'm not to water it until the top third of the pot goes dry. A eucalyptus will grow to six feet in the blink of an eye and when that happens I will have to donate it, but they don't say where. The biggest leaf on my plant is the size of a fifty-cent piece. It's been years since I saw one of those. So far it doesn't smell like a eucalyptus, maybe it's too young, but it is one of five indoor plants that can suck toxins out of the air, which is nice to know, but I don't Google the other four.

Outside my window everything is alive with blooms and bees and the occasional small rabbit for whom I can leave some disappointingly mealy nectarines. Finally something I actually want to do! Fruit in one hand, cane in the other, I manage not to fall down the porch steps, not to trip on the uneven flagstones, not to step on any living thing, and successfully drop the fruit next to some flowers whose name I forget. Now I can watch the action from my chair by the window. I don't expect company soon, but rabbits show up in the evening. The eucalyptus is still leaning toward where the sun used to be because now not only is it suddenly raining, but the sun is headed across the street toward Pennsylvania. Rainbows are good luck. Tomorrow is September first.

How to Do Nothing

CHOOSE A NICE DAY. Or not, rain will do as well. Doing nothing is not meditation. You are not emptying your mind, you are letting it wander around from one thing to another while you sit still. Some people think of monkey mind as something to be conquered, or corralled, or even obliterated, but there is nothing wrong with your monkey mind—let it hang by its tail off the ceiling fan if it wants to. Look, the wind is stirring things up. You will see the ghostly white shapeless thing that has puzzled you all summer, a mystery you couldn't solve because the ground is uneven and the long walk across the acre of yard would likely result in a fall and you would be too far from the house to push the button thing you wear around your neck to call for help. Anyway, with fall, and this stiff wind stripping leaves off everything, that white ghostly thing has begun to take shape, turning slowly day by day and now hour by hour into the old wicker chair. Where did it come from? It sits surrounded by thorny berry bushes. Who dragged it out there and to do what? Your daughter will explain later that she and her sons were looking for birds' nests. Maybe they used it to stand on next to the locust which is also now bare. Next to it, there's a large red object, what could it be? Never mind. Your daughter will know. Check out the ground underneath the hydrangea tree and notice how black and fresh it appears due to the squirrel yesterday burying and digging up and burying and digging up the carrots you left there, notice no carrots visible at the moment, were they eaten? Saved for winter? Hard to know. A little squirrel with OCD. No birds today, it's gray and going to rain but not yet, take a gander at your crazy funny pilea plant on the windowsill which is sticking out in all directions with big bright round leaves, each with a pale belly button where the stem attaches on the back, keep looking, because the longer you do, the longer you smile. Outside, the hydrangea tree blossoms are vanishing into brown shapeless clusters that were fat triangles pointing toward the sky and their shape reminded you of prayers. What god were they thanking? beseeching? Must have been the sun, and now you are thinking about the mist rising in coils off the meadow and it is just one quick step backward to remember spirits inhabiting everything and anything and everywhere alive.

Be careful, the slightest shift in attention, or the lack thereof, will steer you toward crumbling. It's okay to cover your face with your hands, because it feels so good. Anyone watching you now holding your head in your hands might be forgiven for thinking you're in distress, but this is the only comfort available in these days of death and dying and you aren't going to move until the monkey comes back.

Another Wasp

SOMETHING TICKLED MY WRIST JUST NOW and I tried to shake off what I thought might be a spider, but turned out to be a wasp. It must have come in with me when I put the corn out for the critters, latching itself to the sleeve of my purple jacket. It is missing a wing. Now it's crawling up my sleeve, which freaks me out, so after a flurry of activity on my part, the wasp is now sitting on check number 1440 of my checkbook, under a glass. I can carry it outside and let it go, which is what I will certainly do in a minute. In just a minute or two. Meanwhile, I look at it, wondering what instinct has taken over. It is so still. Maybe it is waiting for its lost wing to come back. Maybe it is hiding, the way kids do, by closing their eyes. I don't know. If it were me in there, I'd be screaming and yelling and banging against the walls. If I were missing the human equivalent of a wing, what would that be? an arm? a leg? There is no human equivalent of a wing. Maybe my mind. My imagination would have been severed. No curiosity. No hope. I would be just as still, unable to have a thought, a plan, or any idea of what had happened.

Company is coming soon, or in an hour or two. Company with food, a farewell of sorts to a friend who is moving to Texas. I look forward to their arrival. We will all wear masks and I have the fan on and the windows open. One of them has baked a cake. I have done nothing to welcome them, and I will limp around with my cane so they will understand that I'm not good for much of anything.

The wasp. I can't fix it. I can't make its life workable. It has folded its remaining wing close to its body so it now resembles an ant, a long black ant. Is this a sign of resignation? Is it trying to be small? Does it feel reassured pulling itself close? Does it know it is doomed? I can't keep it. A wasp does not deserve to meet its maker trapped under a glass on my checkbook. Where should I deposit this mortally wounded thing? Maybe the rose of Sharon? It bloomed so extravagantly this year. Maybe the hibiscus, with its red flowers so huge my daughter Jen compares their size to a satellite dish. If it had a voice, this hibiscus, it would boom out its messages. No one would get any sleep. Maybe the hydrangea tree. Oh! A squirrel is making off with one of the corncobs I put there. Two left now.

The wasp is so still. Not a single movement, not a leg twitching, not an antenna shifting, just sitting there under the glass on check number 1440. Motionless. Oh, little wasp. Show a sign of life, show a little irritation. I lift the glass, but it still doesn't move. I am behaving as though it is there for my pleasure, to satisfy some curiosity I just discovered. I have to make a decision. Checkbook, wasp, and glass in place, I grab my cane and take the whole shebang out to the porch, lift the glass, and shake the checkbook over the rose of Sharon. The wasp clings. Oh, hell. This is so hard. Finally I brush it off with the sleeve of my purple jacket, very carefully, so as not to injure it further. I look down through the branches but it has vanished. Good luck, little wasp. I didn't know what else to do.

PART THREE

WISTERIA

The sudden green feather about to adorn its
second wild
Animal, the tender next minute waiting for us
to emerge.

—Brian Doyle, *One Long River of Song*

The Falcon

THE FALCON CATHERINE SAW SITTING on a low branch of my locust blended in so perfectly that it was impossible for me to find it. But it was there, I know, she kept pointing at it. I couldn't see it, no matter how I tried, no matter how I fiddled with the angle of my binoculars. So I'm going to believe that maybe there are things so perfectly camouflaged in the environment that even when I can't see them they are there. And who knows what I will see by not seeing it? A unicorn? A phoenix? rising from its ashes? I will start looking tomorrow. Or now.

Orchids and Mice

JENNIFER GAVE ME TWO ORCHIDS. I love them. The blossoms, trembling on their stems, look like delicate creatures paused midflight. The taller is wildly pink, the smaller, white. I put them on my kitchen counter where I can see them from my chair. I'm supposed to water them with an ice cube. We don't know why, maybe for the slow leak, but it seems cold for such a fragile-looking flower.

The other morning I discovered dirt on the counter, and the white orchid lying on the floor, its little pot broken, the orchid itself intact. I couldn't imagine what had happened. What wayward wind could have blown through my kitchen? I thought maybe it had tipped over from the weight of its flowers. I picked it up, repotted it, and set it back on the counter.

The next morning, in the tall orchid's pot, I discovered some of its dirt scooped out as clinically as if someone had used a sharp-edged object, a grapefruit spoon maybe, leaving a perfectly shaped oval declivity, not a crumb out of place, and dirt sprinkled on the counter. What on earth could have done such a thing? Some mythic beast?

These days, no matter how my day has gone, I am uneasy going to bed. There's no reason for this, and every reason for this. The pandemic, the politics, and once in a while something a little extra. Last night, for example, I heard a door close upstairs. I live with my dogs who were sleeping on the sofa next to me, nobody else in my house, and the unmistakable sound of a door closing was unsettling. This has happened before, and I have learned to accept what I can't explain. Mystery is its own answer.

Paul came over the next day, and found a single mouse turd on the counter.

"A mouse!" I cried. "Just a mouse!"

"Mice," said Paul. "There's never just one."

Paul has had moles (moles!) in his kitchen.

I wish I had moles. I love moles. "No," said Paul, "they are not cute in person."

At night, I put the orchids in the middle of the sink where the mice have not dared to venture. Whatever else might be here, I'm going to live and let live.

The hard thing about going to bed involves my dog Daphne. Sadie follows me, but Daphne hasn't slept with us since the day Cooper died. He was our first responder, keeping vigil on the living room sofa while the rest of us slept in my bed, waking only when we heard his midnight howls. The day Cooper died, Daphne took up his post and has slept there ever since. There are nights when within five minutes of the lights going off, Daphne begins a kind of halfhearted barking. I can hear her as I lie in bed with Sadie. She's not barking at anything in particular, they aren't urgent sounds, they sound sadder, lonelier, forlorn. It's as if she's suddenly discovered that she is alone.

An Invitation

FROM A FEW PEOPLE SHE LOVES and she wanted to go and she was planning to go and even baked a blueberry cake and there is nothing terrifying about them or this sunny afternoon which makes it worse that she can't get herself to move or even make the call.

No More Napping

I LIKE TIME DOTTED WITH ONE THING AND ANOTHER, otherwise the day does its thing without me, without my having used my share. There have been so many hours spent making nothing of interest, doing nothing of use. Time not only passes, it passes me by. I want to be conscious. I don't want to miss anything. There must be something to learn. There must be something to do. Sometimes just for fun I look at the blue sky with both eyes and it's grayish blue, but if I close my left eye, it's that lovely blue. I never went back to fix the other cataract in my left eye. So I take turns, both eyes grayish blue, right eye blue, gray, blue, gray, blue.

Something to Do, or,
Be Careful What You Wish For

I HAVE TOO MUCH STUFF. Objects cover every surface. Books sit in stacks on tables, chairs, the floor. Junk crams cupboards and shelves so completely that my eyes can't distinguish one thing from another. And yet I can never find scissors, or a pen, or rubber bands or paper clips or safety pins, the kinds of things junk drawers are made for. Years ago a friend sent me the galley of a book called *The Gentle Art of Swedish Death Cleaning.* Death cleaning? You mean the sheets? The body fluids released by the deceased? A whole book? It lay unread for years, but now I pick it up. Maybe it will give me something to do. I begin to read and get excited. It's divesting your house of things your kids won't want, things they shouldn't have to paw through, and things you don't want them to find. Thrilled and energized, I get up and throw out the kitchen. Drawers full of things like broken wristwatch bands, pencils snapped in half, cotton balls, unstrung beads. A Le Creuset casserole with black burnt bits still stuck despite a million Brillo pads. Out it goes. Under the table somebody's right sneaker I don't recognize. Worn-out wallets, notebooks, odds and ends of broken tools, marbles, an old driver's license, orphaned bits of Lego, there is so much crap that I stop looking, just upend everything into the rubbish. I throw out things that aren't even mine. "Mother!" cries my daughter Catherine. "How could you throw out Tim's father's old sneakers?" A wooden god of some sort that had lain on the porch for months. I thought nobody would miss it. "Mother. Really? That was Joe's favorite thing!" In no time everything is back where it was before she started. An exercise in futility.

Bat Won't Leave House

Is the headline on a site where Woodstock residents present problems asking for solutions. I'm in love with this stubborn little bat. Bat won't leave house. Oh, please, whoever you are. Let it stay.

Spatchcocking the Chickens

THERE MUST BE SOME UNDERLYING REASON to explain my enthusiasm for spatchcocking a chicken, or chickens, as I have done three already, on different days, of course. The obsession began when my son Ralph sent me a link to a recipe that involved spatchcocking, a word I didn't know. It means to cut the backbone out of a chicken before you cook it. It comes from "dispatching the cock" about which I have no comment, except to say it appeared in *A Classical Dictionary of the Vulgar Tongue*, in 1785, compiled by Captain Francis Grose. I have ordered a reprint of this book, and I can't wait to read it.

I watched the YouTube video, bought a nonstick frying pan and a pair of kitchen shears, picked up a chicken, and came home. I wasn't certain the guys at the butcher had ever heard the word "spatchcock" before, and I didn't want to be the first person to use it in front of them. I planned to spatchcock it myself.

I'm good at chicken, but at my age something new to do in the kitchen sounded exciting. Something new to do, period. Bonus points for anything that takes my mind off whatever is on my mind these days. (I try to avoid the news.) The scissors weren't up to the job, and I had to do a lot of just plain ripping, oh, it was horrible, but strangely satisfying in a primitive kind of way. No, primitive doesn't describe what I felt, savage comes closer. Anyway, after you take out the backbone and cut something vague in the breastbone and flatten it out, the chicken looks a little like an angel and nothing like a chicken. Then you put it skin-side down in a nonstick frying pan, and start it cold over a low flame, gradually turning the flame up until the chicken is cooking in its own fat. Yes, it was the tenderest white meat I've ever had, and yes, the skin was nice and brown although not as brown and crisp as in the video. I realized, after three bites, that I don't really like chicken all that much, at least not when I'm eating it by myself. And cooking something in its own fat sounds like what human beings might have done to torture another human being who would later become a saint. Flayed alive.

At least the chickens were already dead.

However, for reasons I cannot fully explain, as I have already confessed, I have since spatchcocked two more chickens. The second one I shared with the dogs. When the third one was all nice and brown and juicy, I cut up a bunch of carrots, mixed up some dumplings, and made chicken soup. When it was done I ate everything except the chicken. Then, while hunting for the tinfoil to wrap the meat, I realized I hadn't been using the new scissors because there they were, in the way-back of the drawer, which was why the procedure had been so hard, and now having found the real kitchen shears, I can't wait to do it to a turkey! This is nuts. I'm a seventy-nine-year-old barbarian.

What is wrong with me? Why do I keep doing this horrible thing? How to explain this frenzy! My friend Paul suggests the chicken might be a "transitional object," and removing its backbone is the substitute for what I want to cut out of my life but can't bring myself to look at. Well, I can't bear to listen to the news anymore but sometimes I hear it by accident. Or I read a headline before I can stop myself. We are not my favorite animal, although there are many of us I love, and many millions more I fear for. I think Earth is preparing to shrug us off. Ants have been around for at least 168 million years, minding their own business. I looked them up once. We've been here for a measly two hundred thousand, and have done more damage than all other species combined. Okay. I'm facing it. I can think of no solution.

I need a new habit. Or maybe just a different verb. "Ponder" is a nice one, reminiscent of, well, a pond. It sounds peaceful. I will fold my hands, take up pondering. Still water, full of life.

Solitude

I CAN SPEND THE BETTER PART OF AN AFTERNOON waiting patiently for the back of my mind to make its way to the front, where I can discover what I'm thinking about without thinking about anything. Looking up at the trees whose high, thick trunks are swaying ever so slightly in the wind (how can this be?), I want to watch undisturbed for as long as I feel like it, even if it's just a minute or two, even if it leads nowhere. What if I had a soul mate? What if he wandered into this room and offered to make me a sandwich? Would I prefer a roll? ham? mayo? mustard? I would become my least favorite self. The irritable one. Being irritated is like having poison ivy of the bloodstream and I hate it and I hate myself when I feel it. I prefer being the me who lives with dogs.

But a storm is coming. They are predicting gale-force winds. I will hate it if the power goes off and it's cold and dark and my phone won't work and I can't find the hat Ralph gave me, oh, here it is, thank God, still on the ottoman. But still I will be miserable and probably scared to death. The dogs will be bewildered and nervous but they will stay close, all of us will huddle together. They know how to wait it out. They teach me patience.

Oh, good, there's that fat gray bird with a yellow belly again, I've seen it before. The gray is so intense it's almost blue. Such a long slender tail! It hops forward, then back, then forward, then back, again and again, tiny little hops! Now it is sort of ruffling itself in the earth. What for? What is the point? There must be a reason for this activity! Is it just delight? Does it know a storm is coming? Five more birds now, just like the first one, all doing the funny little dance. A family! Dancing! Lucky me.

Wisteria

A SKINNY STICK WITH GNARLY ROOTS set in a glass cylinder of water sat on my desk for months looking about as dead as dead gets. Now it is suddenly alive. Alive and growing! It's a wisteria vine, Catherine bought it for me, and although neither of us held out much hope, the new green leafy stem is growing three and four inches every day. And not only that, but there are now seven other stems with leaves that I swear were not there this morning.

It's like a science fiction movie. I imagine sitting in the living room, looking up to find dozens more branches (because pretty soon they will be branches, not stems) wending their way up the walls and windows, across the ceiling, turning my room into a green cave, hung with lavender-blue blooms.

I watch the wisteria every day. It does have branches now, and a long prehistoric-looking frond that is reaching upward and out, looking for something to attach itself to. It reminds me of the antenna of a living creature, sensing where it is, wondering where next to go. My daughter swears we could probably watch it growing, if we stood still and stared. It seems all its energy is going into the reach, the leaves remain tiny buds on this part of the plant. Any day now, we will find out where it's going. Soon there will be another vine, and another.

My friend Cathy says she thinks there are two kinds of people: those who are willing to take the long way, and those who just want to get there, wherever there happens to be. Cathy lives in Missouri where I have never been; she likes to explore, she likes to take her time, so when she and her husband set off somewhere, to visit her sister maybe, they take the long way. I love this distinction. Which kind of person am I? Where am I going? I'm going back sixty-five years. The place is still there, I could hop in my car and be there in less than two hours. That would be the short way. My fear is that everything might look the same but feel different, and I want to return only to what I remember. That's a different kind of journey.

Wisteria wants to go everywhere at once, those vines will search out every crack, invade every crevice, climb any wall, undermine any foundation. Clinging to whatever it encounters, wisteria overwhelms every other growing thing in its path, all the while festooning the world with those lavender-blue blossoms. This is what my gardener friend Karin warned me about. "It will take over everything," she said, as if this were a bad thing.

We lived in a white house on a bend in the road that wound its way down to the Hudson River, there were tides, streams, a waterfall, woods. There was also a boy. Wisteria grew over my bedroom windows, the fragrance from its trembling blossoms too delicate, too sweet, too tender for words. I think of the boy in the same breath as I think of wisteria, and I'm headed back to a summer afternoon when that boy taught a shy, hesitant fifteen-year-old girl, very gently, what a French kiss felt like. Sixty-five years ago. When my wisteria blooms.

Gratitude

I HATE THOSE SUGGESTIONS that we make "gratitude lists," as if it were some new commodity and we all need to get us some. Gratitude, bah, humbug. I'm beginning to hate the word. Besides, anything and anyone I am grateful for comes dragging a heavy tail of worry or sorrow or both. I am teetering next to a depression that will hang around like a low-grade fever, so I look for something to see, or do. I am losing track of what I am. I hope something small catches my eye, takes me elsewhere. Come to think of it, I'm not crazy about hope either. Hope is simply the precursor to hopes dashed. Hoping for the best? Good luck with that.

Oh, good. My tiny eucalyptus tree needs more dirt. At least I think it does. The base of the trunk appears to be heaving up the dirt surrounding it. (The word "trunk" is a wild overstatement, as it is slender as a bobby pin.) Sitting on my porch is a shiny aluminum garbage can Catherine filled with dirt and compost from the far part of the yard, when the mice were digging holes in my houseplants and I needed to fill them in. So I take a little glass and scoop up a bunch of the rich crumbly black stuff, to arrange evenly around the eucalyptus tree. Next to the tiny trunk I put a blue heart my friend Craig gave me, and the graceful hand of my Virgin Mary garden statue that broke off when a small child embraced her, and she toppled. I keep a close eye on the progress of my tree, but not much happens, or if it does, it is with glacial slowness.

Something flutters onto my shirt, or almost onto my shirt, and I brush it away, with what has become a familiar motion, what with all the bugs that have arrived in the house since the pandemic. There it is on the floor. I put a glass over it, and an envelope under the glass, and take a good look. It's a stinkbug, looking prehistoric, shaped a bit like a shield. I bet it came in with the compost. This is the first one I've seen this year. I love them. They move slowly and deliberately until they find a spot on the wall where they want to stop, and then they do, for long periods of time. Are they meditating? Contemplating their next move? Pretending they are invisible? Loafing? Hibernating? No idea.

I have Googled stinkbugs many times, just to make sure that's what I've got, and am always dismayed to find how many entries there are about how to kill them. I don't want to kill a stinkbug. Mine (I do think of them as mine) have never bothered me, or released their stink, they are quiet companions here one day, somewhere else the next. I love how they take life in such an unhurried fashion. Maybe that's because I see them in the fall, when life slows down for everything. Sometimes dozens and dozens move into houses for winter, attracted by a smell one stinkbug emits, something called an aggregation pheromone. What's the harm? They don't bite, and they don't stink unless you hurt them or scare them. I shake the stinkbug onto the windowsill and watch it sitting still. My sister had an infestation of ladybugs one winter. It was the size and shape of a football, hanging in a corner.

There's nothing lying around but my pound cake. I've got to eat something else, and I've got to get out of the house. It will be dark soon, and I don't drive in the dark. Finally, something urgent. Sadie knows the minute I put my shoes on that I'm leaving, and she is waiting at the car before I'm even out the door. I don't know whether she loves to drive, or if she's afraid I'll disappear forever. God knows I worry about her, as she is now an old girl. There you have it in a nutshell, love and gratitude riding alongside the fever of worry.

There is a line at the butcher, only four customers allowed in at a time, but I'm in luck. There is only one woman ahead of me, although suddenly a lot of others show up and the line behind me is growing. There is probably an algorithm for this. I remain unclear on what an algorithm actually is, but I hear the word bandied about everywhere there are statistics. But it does seem to be a fact of life that there's a lull, then an overload, then a lull. Aggregation pheromones. Do we have them?

My turn. I buy two Campanelli chickens, more buttermilk, two pounds of sweet butter, and a brownie. Do I need help getting the bags to my car? asks the boy behind the counter. I shake my head, say nope, I've got it thanks. Bag in one hand, cane in the other, I'm just about to get the door when an older man opens it for me, and I thank him. My heart is warming up. I try to look sympathetically at the long line still waiting, but it's hard behind a mask, and then Sadie and I drive home.

I put the groceries on the counter and check the windowsill. My stinkbug hasn't moved an inch. And there's still only one of him. So far, so good.

No Bugs, Not Again

THE ONLY TIME I FEEL LIKE MYSELF is when I'm writing. The only time I am invulnerable. Otherwise I am a sitting duck, filled with anxiety about one thing or another, one loved one or another, the planet itself. But how many more times can I write about bugs? They must be getting in through the dog door because the flap fell off months ago. Today appeared one of those slender black winged creatures whose long legs dangle when airborne. It was delicate and quite beautiful in an ominous way. I trapped it under a glass, slid a postcard underneath, and took it outside. I have written about wasps, a firefly, big black ants (one big black ant in particular), and my favorites, of course, the stinkbugs. I have done cluster flies to death. Flies are the only insects I kill. It wasn't until I wrote about spiders that my friend Ann finally put her foot down. "Enough with the bugs," Ann said. But I have to write about something. And the bugs keep coming.

Today, and for several days running, there has been a tiny pale-brown ant crawling around aimlessly on the side of the gray bookcase right next to my chair, oops, it seems to have disappeared. So featureless, so smooth the bookcase, round and round went the ant. Was it looking for landmarks? Was it lost? I wonder what passes for loneliness in an ant. It was right there a second ago, rather a reliable companion. Where did it go? Bug or no bug, I'm curious, so I Google ants. Wow. Ants have been around since before the early Cretaceous Period, more than 145 million years ago. My respect for them grows. We are the newcomers here, an arrogant species, and arrogance is not useful for survival. We are not built to last.

I look again at yesterday's fly, dead on its feet, so to speak, stuck to the thin wooden frame that surrounds a small painting leaning against the window by my chair. The fly looks like a piece of art. It died after I sprayed it with Windex, the only thing I had handy, and it slid down the window feet first, landing on its hind legs, and there it remains, stuck standing up, as if gazing out at the late summer afternoon. Can one say about a fly that it has hind legs? It's the only bug I don't like. Bug. An all-purpose name for a million different creatures. Such a funny little word, "bug." Almost adorable.

The word that obsesses me these days is "ruin." Lowercase. It sounds like what it is, starting with *ru*, as in rue the day. It even looks like its definition: ruin. ruin. ruin. Nothing left standing, nothing toppled sideways or piercing the below, everything brought down, leveled. The end of us. And that dot over the *i*? The last speck of smoke just about to vanish.

The day is over. Thank God I started writing. Lying in bed with my dogs I have one last unwelcome thought. Maybe it isn't smoke.

Maybe it's a fly.

Farmland

LYING IN BED, my dogs still asleep, I was struck by the sprawl of my pandemic body, how much room it takes up, how much surface it covers, maybe almost an acre if everything was evenly distributed. Then an idea: me as an acre of farmland! Soybeans and alfalfa (whatever that is) and orchards for apples and pears and cherries, and vegetable gardens so I never run out of fennel or red onions and somewhere a watermelon patch, and amber waves of grain! Lots of those! I would need, of course, pollinating insects, and some kind of fertilizer. How about grazing animals? That might feel nice. Corn? Lots of corn. What parts of me would be best for sheep? Goats? How many cows? Where would the meadow go? Chickens! Every farm has chickens! And a nice clear stream for irrigation and drinking water and somewhere I'd need to dig a well. And plenty of dogs for herding the sheep and guarding the chickens. Where will everything fit? I don't know what would be best planted on my extremities, they seem useless for farmland. Grapevines? Damn. Maybe sunflowers?

It slowly became clear my body wasn't generous enough for all these plans, and it began to fall back asleep. And what with the cornfields blocking my view, I wouldn't be able to see anything anyway. I was still clear about dogs, lots of dogs, dogs all over, running through the tall grasses, barking and howling and jumping into the stream, drinking the water, shaking and wriggling on their backs, how delicious that would feel. And drifted off again. Eventually my two old dogs woke and crawled out from under the covers, we all slid off the bed, avoiding the fallen produce and livestock, and the day began.

Dread vs. Fear

FEAR MAKES SENSE. Tiger there! Fear tiger! Big teeth! Run away! Even irrational fear makes a kind of sense. We're most of us irrational at one time or another. I looked up "fear" in *The American Heritage Dictionary of Indo-European Roots,* and originally it meant "to try, risk." Perfect. But dread? Dread remains in hiding. It evolved from a root meaning "to count." The word "logarithm" comes from the same root. No clue there. I can't even turn that into a joke.

I've been reading more about phobias. They are so specific as to be almost alluring. They render ordinary fear almost comforting. Take trypophobia, for instance: the fear of holes. Good God! Holes are everywhere: eyelet curtains, sponges, chicken wire, missing teeth—imagine shuddering at a sieve, fleeing from a strawberry. Maybe it's time to count my blessings.

To count. Ah.

My friend Paula, whose imagination has a wider embrace, suggested that counting is born from anxiety. It has taken me three days, but I finally understand.

Four children, twelve grandchildren, that enormous wave, did they all come through when it broke? Two sisters, one nephew, one niece, my friends? Were they in the water? Wave after wave! Who can I count on to take care of my dogs when I die?

Why Can't I Leave My House?

I KEEP WAITING TO BE ABLE TO LEAVE. What will it take? I tell myself it's no big deal, just put your shoes on and get in the car, but then I remember it's chilly today and it's warm here in my chair. I tell myself but you have no food and I answer I'll make French toast, but then I remember I'm out of syrup and don't want French toast, I had that yesterday and the day before and there's no bread left and all the eggs are gone. I tell myself how easy it is to pick up a chicken at the butcher, but I am filled with dread AGAIN and don't need a reason not to go. Because that's my reason.

Am I suddenly becoming one of those sad people who is afraid to leave the house? What is it called? I can only think of claustrophobia because I know I have that, I just don't have it right now. I have the other one. Agoraphobia. That's it. Is this what's happening? Maybe spending so many months in my house has created a centrifugal force pinning me to my chair. I've got to get out of here. So I look up "wait" in my Indo-European dictionary hoping for a little enlightenment and find its earliest root comes from a word for "strong." I beg to disagree. Waiting is hard. It's harder than knowing. Harder than going. But it doesn't require strength, God knows. Maybe endurance. But why endure what I can fix simply by driving into town? It's worse than that. Today I didn't walk down the driveway to pick up the mail. I didn't even stand on my porch.

This time I get as far as the car before I stop. I stand there, the keys in my hand, then turn around and go back up the porch steps, into the house, take up my place in the chair. Nonchalant. As if nothing just happened. But something did. What happened was I didn't go.

Two Days Later

FINALLY. I DON'T KNOW HOW I DID IT. I must have grabbed hold of a moment when my mind was blank, and made it into the car before I could think. Sadie riding shotgun. Once I arrived at Woodstock Meats, I went crazy. I bought an enormous leg of lamb I will never eat, it's as long as my arm, a nice man had to carry it to the car for me. I bought parsnips and onions to cook with it, and I will call Catherine to come get it for her family. I did not buy a chicken, figuring enough was enough. I bought a bottle of ketchup. I'm still out of milk and bread and eggs. I'm low on butter and I'm almost out of dog food. It's pouring now, and I can't go out until tomorrow, but having completed a successful trip into the world and back, I think agoraphobia was a wild overstatement, a dramatic conclusion I jumped to, or else I nipped it in the bud.

Anyway, I'm back in my chair by the window again.

Dream

THERE WAS A VERY CUTE BAD BOY and we loved bad boys and we were all crazy about him, staring and talking and giggling and carrying on, but what I remember best is a sort of dowdy overweight girl whispering to me, "I'm even in love with his shadow."

What Is Wrong with Me?

IT'S SEVEN-THIRTY IN THE MORNING and I'm already tired. My stomach hurts. Too much coffee. The dogs are napping after their wild foray outside. I'm depressed about being tired all the time until I notice the lighter is right there on the table and I don't have to get up to light my cigarette on the stove. I can use the coffee cup as an ashtray, which is one of my disgusting habits. What is wrong with me? Last night a friend slept over, and brought Chinese food and I wasn't going to eat it because he's dead broke, but this was duck and I kept looking at the dark strips and finally he offered me a few which I ate. Then I wanted all of it plus the water chestnuts and broccoli so when he went outside to call his son I gobbled more. He would have been happy to give it to me, but sometimes it is more interesting to feel as if you're doing something sneaky and bad.

Death

MAYBE IT'S TIME TO THINK REALISTICALLY about death. But death is hard to fathom, so I come at it sideways. I do what I usually do when I'm curious or stumped, I grab *The American Heritage Dictionary of Indo-European Roots* to see if the word "dead" began differently. The word "miracle" comes from a root that originally meant "to laugh, to smile," and I've always loved that. If dead evolved from something else, maybe I can evolve along with it, take the ride humankind took, the long way round to face a fact. So although I can't find my glasses and the light is dim, I read that dead came from the Indo-European root "dheu3," and I flip back to the roots section and for one brief ecstatic moment I think that dead evolved from the verb "to flow; to rise in a cloud." How my spirit soars. What a fantastic surprise. I can get behind that, flowing out an open window and evaporating like mist. It is so much more appealing than the cold hard fact of dead. I'm having such a good time now that I look again only to discover that I mistook "dheu2" for "dheu3," and damn it, dead has always been just dead. Of course it has. Dead is dead is dead and there's no story here. I want to end this conversation, I want to change the subject but I can't. I want to think about dying, I want to face facts. One day I will be dead as a doornail, and what will that be like? Well, I'll be dead, so all I can do is try to think about what I think about that. "Dead" is an ugly word. I don't mind "death," it rhymes with "breath," even if it's the last.

Here is a day I would rather forget, I bring it up only because it was mysterious, and has something to do with death. I was settling into my favorite chair in my favorite room, a room filled with various things I've picked up over a lifetime, memories attached to everything, pleasure everywhere, the only difference now was that suddenly nothing meant anything at all. I don't remember how long this lasted, but "numb" is too strong a word for the nothing that I felt. Last summer I had what was later determined to be "a cardiac event." In the middle of a conversation with two nice men about how to help my ailing locust and the ratty-looking crabapple, I fell flat on my face in the yard. I woke up in an ambulance, in a very good mood, with no idea what I was doing there, trying to remember, without having been asked, which (if any) of my three husbands might still be alive.

It wasn't until later that I learned details of what had happened. When I dropped, I'm told my dog Sadie lay down next to me. The two men, Freddy and Angelo, didn't want to move me lest I had broken something. Fred sat down next to me, talking gently and stroking my back. Angelo looked at my phone to see who had last called me, and called that number, getting my sister. Someone called the ambulance. They then rounded up my two dogs, got them in the house, and shut the door. (No easy job, that.) Everything that needed doing was done, and I am profoundly grateful.

But here's what amazes me. I don't recall anything. It's as if I hadn't even been there. I find it oddly comforting. If death is like this, the absence of self, what's the big deal? Unable to resist a little irony, I think I can handle that.

I want my children to get on well without me. I want them to be fine, with good useful lives, remembering me with affection and laughter and some residual irritation or anger or resentment they will work through. I don't want to hang around as a ghost or a rabbit or another human being. And since my first impression is often what sticks, no matter how wrong it turns out to be, I plan to flow out the open window, and evaporate like mist.

For Some Unknown Reason

I AM WEARING LIPSTICK TODAY. I never wear lipstick anymore. My grandson Augie, one of Catherine's boys, is here for a visit. He looks at me accusingly.

"Nana! You are wearing lipstick!"

I hem and haw, saying yes, I borrowed some from his mother. I really can't explain it even to myself.

"Nana!" he says. "Your lips are a lie!"

These Dogs I Love

THE DOGS AND I WAKE WHEN THE SUN COMES UP, we are all excited today. The dogs tumble all over themselves to be first down the porch steps and into the yard. Tails high, noses to the ground, following trails I can't possibly see, the dogs veer left, right, straight ahead, circle back around, occasionally stopping short to pay close attention to something I'd rather not know about (but probably will), lifting their heads to bark or howl, and they are displaying the kind of excited behavior I am myself today.

I've been writing something I don't understand yet, and what I'm following (or being led by) might have laid down its tracks fifty years ago, or yesterday. If you could map my mind, it would resemble the zigzagging dogs prints in an inch of snow: How I spent my allowance in New Orleans? The waterfall in Sneden's? The boy in New Hampshire? It might be anything, but my whole life has brought me here. That's what's so interesting about writing. I veer left, then right, then straight ahead, stopping occasionally to examine something more closely. The only difference is that I do not then roll in it.

There's no telling where I'll wind up, or even if it will amount to anything, but right now, that doesn't matter. Something very interesting might show up at any moment, as long as I keep at it, as long as I don't boss it around, as long as my luck holds. It's all about discovery, it's all about the possibilities. Possibility is a physical sensation, and there's nothing like it. I remember the first time I felt its thrill, listening to my father describe something that was going well in his lab, and although I had no idea what he was talking about, and it hadn't happened yet, he fairly trembled with excitement and his voice contained a tremor I think of now as the awareness of possibility. Oh, I must have thought without thinking, that's the way I want to live. On the brink! Right around the corner! Any minute now!

It's like being a dog. The minute they wake up, when they jump out of bed or slide off the couch, their tails are already wagging. They are expecting the next good thing. On the brink. Right around the corner. Any minute now.

Wisteria: An Update

ONE OF THE WISTERIA VINES STRETCHES almost across the kitchen. It goes just so far, then the tip curls back around itself, latching on to nothing but thin air. It waves and trembles. It's like an animal, with instincts. I brush against it when I go back and forth. In a different mood, this could almost be frightening, but its motive is life, not harm, and the leafy branches are quite beautiful.

I have spent the past year in this house, most of it in this chair. The weeks come and go, the sun rises and sets, the days are long then short then long again, and none of it means a thing to me anymore. I don't even remember what I'm missing. The wisteria is a new way of measuring time. The vines! Now that I can watch its progress day by day, sometimes almost hour by hour, I can experience time passing. And at least something in this house is getting somewhere.

But I'm going to move the whole shebang off the kitchen counter to my window. It is almost painful to watch this vine looking for a place to get busy. I keep imagining a human hand opening and closing on nothing at all. There is an old wooden swordfish hanging in front of the window by my chair, a decent destination. By the next afternoon the vines are spilling over the back of the swordfish, curling round and round on themselves, in two separate spirals. They look like joy. The wisteria has found a place to begin.

Catherine is impressed. She spent the night as she sometimes does. I love her company. "Wow, Mom," she says. "That's amazing." She is fixing herself a cup of tea.

"When it gets too big, I'm going to plant it right outside my window," I tell her.

"It will destroy the house, Mom," she says, "You can't plant it there."

"But I'll be dead before the house is destroyed," I say.

"I don't want the house destroyed," she says, her voice rising a little. "Plant it by that tree." She points to the locust.

"That's my favorite tree," I say. "That's my locust." Catherine is now peering inside my icebox. "Oh God, I'm sorry I'm out of milk," I say. "And I think that's gone bad." She is holding a quart of half-and-half.

"I think it's okay, it hasn't even been opened. How about over by the slide?" she suggests, opening it, taking a sniff, pouring a little into her tea.

"Oh, that's a great idea!" I say. "Perfect!"

After she leaves for work, I think about the slide. Catherine has twin boys, Augie and Fred; Jennifer has twins, Ralphie and Violet. They have known each other since forever. It's more than a slide, it's a swing set, a rock-climbing wall, a ladder, and a turret. When they were little, Jen would drive from Boston to Woodstock on holidays and all four kids played on the swings. They learned how to pump themselves into the sky, how to climb the ladder and slide down the slide, they played on the turret. Because of the pandemic it's been a long time since I saw any of them, or they each other.

They are all teenagers now, Jen's kids six months older than their cousins. The last time they were all here together, they would loll on the swings, twirling them a little, their long legs dawdling the dirt beneath them, bowing their heads to talk about God knows what, I'd hear the occasional burst of laughter. That seems a million years ago. Maybe when we are all able to get together again, the wisteria will have covered the structure, making a jungle they can explore (unless they are too cool). Oh God, I miss them so badly, I haven't let myself feel it until now. Wisteria doing double duty.

Birthday Plans

I'LL BE EIGHTY SOON. Maybe I should think about a party. I'm going to want a party, but I don't want to plan it, I'll just tell everyone that I want one and see what happens.

That's three "wants" in two sentences, but I'm too busy to fix it. The only time I planned a party for my birthday was when I turned forty, 1981. That was a good one. There was dancing and I'm (was) a good dancer. The dirty bop. Chuck was horrified. He asked me a question I can't remember anymore. I forget who my boyfriend was back then. Tom? Was it Tom? I don't think so. It was either before or after Tom, but I'll be damned if I can remember which. He left a notebook open once when he was living with me temporarily and I read just one line, although I can't remember exactly whether it was "Everybody loves Abby but nobody wants her," or "Everybody wants Abby but nobody loves her." I never read another word he wrote, although he was a writer and I worked for his editor. I also never told him. Once I read a line from my youngest daughter's homework assignment notebook, she left it open on the kitchen table turned to a page that read, "Elizabeth and I are going to drop acid this weekend." She was in high school. That didn't end well either. And that was the last time I read anything that anyone left lying around. Getting back to my birthday. I'm going to want a cake with roses on it and vanilla ice cream to go on top. I will want my whole big family, and their dogs. It might not be too cold, we can sit outside. I will want everybody from my workshops and I want them all to have the best time ever, and also my friends. It's my last chance. Because what's eighty-one? It doesn't have nearly the dignity of eighty.

Tattoo

Sᴉxᴛʏ. It sounded so substantial, so respectably old, a milestone, and I wanted to mark the place. Get a tattoo popped into my head out of nowhere. Perfect. I would get my first tattoo. It would be a salamander, because I love the way they look, and how they feel like a little puddle of mercury in the palm of your hand, and plus they are magic. A young friend, Rachel, asked to come along and maybe get one for herself, so before we could chicken out, we dropped everything and hotfooted over to St. Mark's Place right into a tattoo parlor. While we waited our turn, we stared at a young man who was having extravagant wings tattooed all across his back. It seemed a shame. So beautiful! Who would see it?

We wondered how painful this was going to be. "Do you think it will hurt as much as having a baby?" Rachel asked. I didn't know. She thought for a moment. "Do you think it will hurt as much as a really bad farming accident?" she asked. I have forgotten her last name and what she had tattooed, but I've never forgotten that perfect question.

I'm getting a second tattoo in honor of turning eighty. The whole phrase is too much to tolerate if it hurts as much as my salamander did, so it's just going to be initials. Black, I think, a nice severe black. It will go on my left arm, because the salamander lives on my right. At first I wanted the font from the *New York Times* but it's too complex. I settled on simple capital letters, like scrabble squares. FTS. It stands for Fuck This Shit.

There are two tattoo parlors right in town. I'm going to the one that opens at noon because it says first come, first served. I arrive on time, but there's already a wait, so I wander around, looking at all the options. There is a wonderfully menacing snake that could fit comfortably on my left arm, and there are delicate feathers in delicate hues, but I stick to my guns. FTS means something to me, the other images are merely beautiful. I adopted Fuck This Shit as my motto during the Trump administration and find it applies to something new every day.

I'm next in line. The artist is a lovely young woman with black braids and tattoos all over her arms. She has listened carefully to what I want, and is off to make a stencil of the letters. I wanted to figure out what that vine is on her left arm, and those creatures, but she's already gone.

I sit down to wait on a bench by the window while the little room fills with more young people. It's a summer Saturday in Woodstock. A couple arriving on a motorcycle want a pair of tattoos like puzzle pieces that fit together, one on her arm, one on his. A young woman sitting near me is having a serious discussion about the pros and cons of getting a tattoo if you're female and may want to run for president someday. "The press would be all over me," she says, "because I'm a woman." Her friend points out that if the tattoo goes on her ankle she can cover it with a sock. Or on her arm, she can wear long sleeves. More discussion. As far as I can tell, this is not a frivolous conversation. We have come some distance if a young woman is going to defer getting a tattoo until she decides whether or not to run for the presidency.

The only tattoos I've seen so far are on the artists, who appear from time to time to see if anyone is serious about an appointment. Tattoos cover every inch of their visible skin. I wonder what it's like to make art with such a limited shelf life. Maybe they also paint on canvas. The motorcycle couple leaves, deterred by the cost of tattoos when you add color.

The young woman is back to show me the letters she has made into a stencil for my approval, ushers me into the room where the work goes on, and points me to a massage-type table where I am to lie down with my arm stretched out on a little extension. She asks me to take off my watch. Then she transfers the letters to my left arm, and proceeds to tattoo them in. I don't watch and I barely feel a thing and it is over in no time. I wonder why she is so quiet. It turns out she is upset because the ink of the *F* is blurred, and she worries it might not disappear. "Your skin is so thin," she explains, apologizing, "Please come back in a week if it doesn't look right by then." I tell her I don't mind, and give her a big tip. I love it. The imperfection is perfect. Because FTS.

They are so young, these artists. Already covered with art. What will they do when they run out of canvas? When every square inch of their body is taken? Then in ten years or fifty they see a bird they've never seen before or a blue they have to have, or a green. What then?

I think I may go back for the snake, or the feather. Or both. I'm not running for anything. Or maybe I'll just wander around.

Time Passing Me By

I LEFT MY WATCH AT THE TATTOO PARLOR and now it's closed and I have to wait three days before it reopens. I miss it so much. It's a Timex from CVS. Big face, real numbers. I keep trying to check the time and my watch keeps not being there. I can't stop, it used to be a reflex. Now it's an obsession. Why should I care? I eat when I'm hungry, I sleep when I can no longer keep my eyes open, nothing requires my timely attendance except the two workshops I give every week. Mondays at six, Thursdays at three. But time is so spooky, because where does it go when it's gone? You have to keep an eye on it. Some weeks there aren't even any Tuesdays! There, I just checked my empty wrist again. Nothing. FTS. I need my watch. I really need my watch. Thank God CVS is open. I hop in the car.

It's 2:29. Now it's 2:33. And so forth.

She Finds This Death
Buried in the Red Folder

WHEN HE WOKE AGAIN HE QUESTIONED how had he come to be here in this terrible room, this room meant for the dying, who had allowed it to happen? And he raged at his wife for betraying him, and when in her pained look he could read nothing he understood, I should never have trusted you, he said, and went on that way like a bath overflowing until his voice softened, I loved you passionately, always, and let his head fall back on the pillow. She wasn't his wife anymore, but she would always be his wife. She took his hand when he startled, his eyes rolling like a wild horse, and he wanted to say she need not trouble herself, as it was only a moment and gone, part of the hard work of it. The body that held him to the bed was loosening its hold and he scattered and filled the room. I love you, his not wife whispered as he died, and the family woke and rose and stood about the bed, weeping, while over by the window a glass of water fell to the floor, which was good-bye and god-damn and he knew she knew, because she almost smiled.

Offering

A COUPLE OF WEEKS HAVE GONE BY since I left food out for the rabbits and squirrels and whatever else came looking, and the days are short and colder now. Yesterday late afternoon I found three apples in the back of the icebox, behind some ancient milk and a skinny bottle of capers. God knows how long they'd lain there forgotten. I cut each apple in half, gathered up a bunch of fat carrots and the feathery tops of some fennel, and took it all outside to drop under the hydrangea tree. Then I returned to my post in the chair. I watched out my window until it got dark, there were no takers, and I gave up. But, oh, this morning when I looked again not a scrap remains, and the bare earth feels like a blessing.

An Interesting Question

A FRIEND ASKS ME AN INTERESTING QUESTION. What were you once certain of, she wants to know, that you can no longer count on. I love the question, but for the life of me, I don't have an answer. I was never certain of anything. I was never certain things would work out for the best, or that everything happens for a reason, or that there was some guiding force in my life. Basically I was driving blind for years, dealing with whatever the moment offered or snatched away.

But what could I count on? There must have been something. I think harder. I could count on my body. I could count on strength and endurance and appetites. I could carry and I could lift and I could get a good night's sleep. I could get pregnant and have four children. I could walk the ninety blocks home and climb thirteen flights of stairs. I could stay up all night with a man and be across town at my desk in the morning. My body breathed and digested, everything worked without a hitch. If it wanted doing, my body could do it.

Now I walk with a cane, I avoid stairs, uneven ground deters me. And that dune at Head of the Meadow? Forget it. I'll be eighty next week. My life is quiet now. The last bit of excitement was that unstoppable deluge of morning pee before I could get to the bathroom. I admit it was thrilling, losing control so extravagantly. It had been a while since my body let loose. As I said, I bought Depends that afternoon.

There are people I love. Love and grief go together. My body holds what it can, what it has to. I can still make coffee, light a cigarette, write.

Birthday

IT'S A NICE FALL DAY, AND WE SIT OUTSIDE. All four of my kids, six of my twelve grandchildren, my great-granddaughter, two spouses, a couple of extra dogs. Daphne has vanished upstairs, but Sadie is nervous, and she sticks close. Chuck is here too, his daughter Hannah and her husband Gabe drove him over, he isn't well. We save him the wicker chair, and I bring a pillow from my bed to soften the seat. Then I settle next to him, my legs crossed, and Sadie rests, or more accurately, positions her chin on my dangling right foot, and holds it there. Minutes pass. My son looks over at her, smiling. "It isn't comfortable, but it's necessary," he says. It seems to me this is a statement that can apply to a lot of life: It isn't comfortable, but it's necessary.

At eighty you don't expect to learn something new, at least not every day. However, I am learning something new every day. Granted, it's the same thing, but I learn it over and over with the same startled awareness. I look out at the lush green expanse behind my house, gazing with pleasure at everything growing, especially my locust, loving the spread of its branches, and at the same moment, or a moment later, I remember this is not really my green yard, and not really my tree. Mine to appreciate, to care for while I live, but I don't really own anything. What is mine to keep? Secrets, maybe. Nothing else. Mortality is hitting home in interesting ways, but it doesn't diminish the pleasure I take in the way my locust fills the sky—my locust, old habits die hard.

Dead

1.

HOW MANY TIMES have I looked up that word in my *Dictionary of Indo-European Roots*? Three, believe it or not. Always the same outcome. I mistake "dheu1" for "dheu3," and read "to rise in a cloud." I feel joyous, even triumphant, then realize my mistake. Three times, always the same outcome, outcomes, plural. As if I'd never done it before. "Dheu3" means dead. Dead has always been just dead. Of course it has. I want its origins to be to rise in a cloud. I want humankind to have forgotten what it once knew, back when we were closer to the earth. I want to make a poem out of it. I want it to be a poem. But it isn't. It just isn't.

2.

IF CHUCK COULD COME BACK JUST FOR A MINUTE or maybe in a dream, he'd straighten me out or make me laugh, or both. Probably both. He could always untangle anything, produce clarity out of my most inarticulate muddles. Grief is a muddle. There is comfort in clarity. He would know what to say. He wouldn't even have to think, the words would just be there. Because I have no idea what to do with myself.

So I've been looking for those old poems. The fact that I might never find them again is as frightening as if a large wild bird had just flown into the room. I just had them last night, but that's always when I lose things—when I just had them. I look on the floor, in the drawers of the little chest by my chair, I rummage through the wastebasket. I smoke two cigarettes. The day darkens. The dogs stretch.

I look again through the red folder, everything typed on a typewriter, the paper brittle, old poems about lunches we ate together, not very good, but they mean something to me. Finally I find the one I was looking for, "1 Bud, 1 Pack Cheez Doodles," and it's like being back at the beginning instead of the end.

1 Bud, 1 Pack Cheez Doodles (1979)

A jazz band today, they pass
the hat too soon, pack up
after one song, we don't
give them any money. I eat
Chuck's Cheez Doodles.
At one-thirty, the sun slips behind
The Plaza, and we move north
on the grass while an old man
rummages in the garbage can
eating food off wrappers
and a girl goes to pieces
on the steps by General
Sherman. Sometimes we guess
at what went wrong with New York,
but not today. The sky is
a perfect blue, a popcorn day.
Last week we walked across town
and stood where somebody had calculated
an enemy bomb would fall
and Chuck told me how far
they figured a runner could get
in twenty minutes headed
uptown. A blond woman in magenta
stockings sits down next to us,
she reads *Principles of Accounting*.
We walk slowly back to work,
our love where it belongs, jingling
in our pockets like loose change.

Home

Usually I am comfortable here, completely at home with myself, although I admit to a bit of a turn when I realized as my eye went easy over things I love in the room where I sit, that one day this will all be stripped from the walls and dispersed, because I will be dead and the house will belong to somebody else, and their stuff will go up on the walls, and fill these rooms. I did feel a bit odd, as if everything I love was suddenly at an unfamiliar angle, but I got over it pretty quickly. Eighty will do that for you. And over there is the candied-apple-red urn Chuck gave me. Having decided that's where I'll be, I can gaze across the room at my final dwelling, and from time to time, depending on the news, almost look forward to the move.

Still Life

APPLES SPILLING OUT OF A BOWL. Sunflowers in a vase. A stack of heavy white plates. Five snow globes arranged on a windowsill. Each one a still life. There are even paintings of fish lying dead on a table. More than one fish, more than one painting. I stare, wondering what possessed an artist to choose dead fish as a subject, but that opens an enormous can of worms because why does anyone decide to explore anything? I need to keep an open mind, except this isn't research. My interest barely rises to the level of a whim. It stemmed from the notion that any depiction of me these days could be called a still life, as I've been sitting in this chair for two years and counting. Paul reminds me that there is no such thing as a still anything, and he brings up Einstein, and molecules, but I can't wrap my mind around that. I feel myself becoming an inanimate object, petrifying, like wood, after so much time in my chair. Paul now informs me there is no such thing as time, just as there is no such thing as stillness. Molecules again. No argument here. Time is a mystery. It disappears, comes back, disappears again, all the while it's still here. Or something is. You'd think it would make some sort of noise, a humming, maybe, or a series of light taps when one moment ends and the next begins. No such luck. I make myself an iced coffee. Oh well, I tell myself, and look out the window. The dogs are chasing that fawn and its mother again. I love how careful they are never to catch them.

PART FOUR

A FEW THOUGHTS
ABOUT WRITING

Choices

I've always been curious about why one chooses fiction for one story and nonfiction for another. For me it's pretty simple—some stories need to be served straight up. That's nonfiction. Others need more architecture, that's fiction. It's a decision best left to the gut. It has been a long time since I wrote fiction, it felt like flying when it went well, but then so does everything; it was thrilling to go chasing some bright scrap of cloth, or a pregnant Dalmatian, or a wild goose, but sooner or later, once I'd had my fun, I'd have to put a roof over its head, give it a place to live and a reason for existing.

Nonfiction comes easily. When something catches my eye, or keeps cropping up, I write. I've been at this long enough to know that the next interesting thing often shows up in disguise, a bug, say, or a certain shade of blue, or a joke someone told that wasn't funny. These bits and pieces don't have to get dressed up for the occasion. I am distilling, not decorating. All I have to do is get it down and get it right. Get in and get out. It's when I'm not quite hitting the bull's-eye that I am flummoxed. There are any number of fragments I have brooded over for days, trying to find that elusive missing bit, needing to get rid of the unsatisfied feeling when I read it aloud to myself. I'm better at cutting. My friend Chuck used to call me the samurai editor.

I love the word "fragment." It has a jagged quality. I looked it up in my copy of *The American Heritage Dictionary of Indo-European Roots* and found it's a straight shot back to the beginning, because its ancestor, "bhreg," meant "to break." I'm not sure writing is our way of fixing what's broken, although that's often a by-product of writing. Sometimes the word "fragment" could be more accurately defined as "shrapnel," and the trick is to determine where the pain originates, remove the foreign object with surgical precision, and see what it is. Painful, but it's part of the deal.

I never know if what I'm writing will add up to anything but I'm always curious to see where my mind goes when it's off-leash. What does it stop to inspect, what does it return to? What the hell am I doing? What are all these memories doing in here? Then there's a physical rush, like falling in love, when what I'm doing begins to reveal itself. I had my eightieth birthday in 2021. What am I up to? I'm an old woman picking up the pieces of her day, wondering where they might lead, loving the journey.

Starting

I LONGED TO BE A WRITER. How did anybody do it? Who was I? I thought a real writer had something to say, something important, and serious; I didn't know anything that mattered. Worse, I couldn't make a story come together in my head. Where to start? How to finish? My problem was I was trying too hard and giving up too quickly. My problem was I thought you had to know what you were doing. Nonsense. You just have to start.

I give assignments in my writing classes because it's hard to make something up out of a clear blue sky. Two pages is all I ask, and it doesn't have to be a story. It doesn't have to be an anything. It can contain a character who shows up out of breath. It can contain a lake and a bunch of swans. There can be conversation or silence. It can take place entirely in the dark. I have learned we do better when we're not trying so hard—there is nothing more deadening to creativity than the grim determination to write a story. At the very least, assignments can provide a writer with a nicely stocked larder, and some notion of where the mind goes when it's off its leash. And once in a while, if we're lucky, an assignment helps you find the side door into a story you've been staring too directly in the eye.

Write two pages that begin with the sentence: "This is a lie I've told before."

Good luck.

Chronology?

I've written memoir for years now in spite of a poor memory. Maybe because of my poor memory. I remember moments, but not necessarily what happened when or what came after. Most of my memories are freestanding. I think of them as dots, like punctuation. Or maybe exclamation points. What year was my second divorce? How was it I left that little school? When did our mother die? I'd have to call my sister and endure the scorn of one with total recall. My memory is full of gaps and tiny holes. But even if I remembered everything in its proper sequence, there's a lot of life that's interesting to live but not so interesting to write about, let alone read. I'm bored by chronology. I don't even believe in chronology. Time is too weird. It contracts, then it shoots forward (or back), it dawdles, stops still, and then suddenly we're twenty years down the road. Whole decades evaporate. Anyway, knowing the sequence of the dots is not as absorbing as the dots themselves. Why these moments? Why not the millions of others? Why now? What to do with them? The trick is not to boss them around. If I am patient, if I call it a day, they move about unobserved, assembling constellations while I sleep.

Total Recall

THANK GOD I AM NOT CURSED WITH TOTAL RECALL. I can see myself stuck inside my steel trap of a memory, rattling the bars, hoping something would shake loose, some scrap I could look at all by itself, something to free me up. Life isn't a puzzle that needs to fit together perfectly, every piece locking into place with every other piece to form a perfect whole. Life is complicated. Stuff overlaps. Some stuff will never fit into one place. Where, for instance, do you stick embarrassment? How do you confine your sense of humor?

But what if I can't remember anything? Well, memories survive on a wisp of fragrance, or a particular shade of blue, or a song that reminds you of a song, so keep your senses open. Follow the details. Detail is the antidote to boredom, and tends to keep depression at bay.

Motive for Memoir

MEMOIR IS NOT A PLACE TO GET REVENGE, or to appear angelic, or to cast oneself as victim. If that's on your mind, write fiction. Memoir should not be self-serving, even accidentally. If you come out as anything but profoundly human, you've probably got the wrong motives for doing this, or you haven't stood far enough back, or come close enough. If you end up where you started—that is, if you wind up with the same feelings about yourself and your life that you had going into this—well, you may not have looked hard enough.

It's about clarity. Clarity usually involves a good deal more humility than you started out with. And humility is accompanied by generosity. And clarity is dependent on a generosity of vision. I'm not saying we let villains off the hook. There is evil out there. I'm just saying a shift in the way we look at ourselves and our lives is one of the benefits of writing memoir. So keep an open mind, leave room for surprise.

Correction

AGES AGO I WROTE AN ESSAY about not feeling guilty anymore—about having had the guilt burnt out of me. It was a proud piece, and rather strident in its claims, but when I read it aloud to myself my voice went dead. I showed it to a friend. "What's wrong with this?" I asked. "Why isn't it working?" He read it and handed it back. "Because it's not about feeling not guilty," he said. "It's about feeling guilty as hell."

Bingo!

I went back to it and learned something.

Hold Your Ground

WHEN I BEGAN WRITING *Safekeeping* I had no idea in hell what I was doing; all I knew was I couldn't stop. What were these little pieces I was feverishly scribbling? They had started coming a few weeks after an old friend died, a man I'd been married to once upon a time, someone I'd known half my life. Memories, moments, scenes, nothing longer than a page or two, some were only a couple of lines. There was no narrative flow. There was no narrative at all. But these bits and pieces kept flying out of me, and I kept writing them down. I left out long boring patches of life I could barely recall. I left out jobs, shrink appointments, lousy boyfriends. I left out a scene that contained two naked people and a scimitar. But I still found plenty to write. I changed voices from first to third to second when it felt right. I mixed up past and present. There was no chronological sense to it, no order. It was popcorn. My sister Judy and I drank a lot of coffee and I would show her what I was writing and when she thought there was more going on than I'd gotten at, she insisted I look harder. She was pitiless. She knew me, she knew about my life. She knew the people I was writing about, and she knew how to corner me. She taught me that too much self-criticism makes for a narrow mind. She could put me in context, seeing me as part of the times we'd lived through, a perspective I didn't have. I used our conversations verbatim. They provide a running commentary on the process of writing. My sister is smart and very funny. She still makes me laugh my head off. The only thing I was sure of was that I would stop with my friend's death. Grief had been the catalyst, grief would be the end. But I hadn't died. Everywhere around me life went on. My eldest daughter had a daughter, and she named her after me, an honor I didn't feel worthy of. My grandmotherly visit was painful, guilt-ridden, but it contained a miracle, and when I realized that this was where I wanted to end, I began to see a kind of emotional chronology. The pieces tumbled back and forth, but something was evolving. My editor turned it down. She wanted me to write a novel about that marriage, what went wrong, what went right, then friendship, illness, and death. But I didn't want to write a novel. My life didn't feel like a novel. It felt like a million moments. I didn't want to make anything fit together. I didn't want to make anything up. I didn't want it to make sense the way I understand a novel to make a kind of sense. I didn't want anywhere to hide. I didn't want to be able to duck. I wanted the shock of truth. I wanted moments that felt like body blows. I wanted moments of pure hilarity, connected to nothing that came before or after. I wanted it to feel like the way I've lived my life. And I wanted to tell the truth. My truth doesn't travel in a straight line, it zigzags, detours, doubles back. Most truths I have to learn over and over again. Every editor in New York turned the little book down except one, Robin Desser at Knopf. That book is twenty-one years old now, and still in print. And most truths I still have to learn over and over again.

The Necessity of Fiction

WHEN I FIRST STARTED TRYING TO WRITE, my subject was myself. I was the only thing I knew anything about, and it wasn't much. My main claim to fame was having been kicked out of college my freshman year for being pregnant in 1959. I married my boyfriend (who didn't get kicked out) and we spent an unhappy eight years together. We were too young to be married to anybody—he was nineteen and I was eighteen, but I think we were particularly unskilled and naïve. We were self-conscious in our new roles—husband, wife, father, mother—and we were either ridiculously polite or we were fighting. But it was what I knew, and it was what I wanted to write about. I started with an evening I remembered pretty well—I was in the kitchen, stirring the beginnings of baked Indian pudding, and my husband came in and said something and we had a big fight. The scene was easily reduced to I did this and he said that and I threw this and he threw that. It all mattered to me, but when I'd written four pages and read it over, I realized that what had been stored in my memory as a vivid crucial scene was whiny and boring. Worse, this wasn't writing, this was tattling. Not knowing what else to do, I put it all away. Years later I wrote other stories, a few about a young couple who found themselves caught in the same circumstances as we had been, but the couple bore no resemblance to either my first husband or me. The characters nagged at me, the situation nagged at me, either I wasn't done with it, or it wasn't done with me. I realized that if I wanted to keep at it, if I wanted to write something longer about a couple of teenagers thrust into a life that was way over their heads, I would have to throw myself a curve. So I made the young wife in love with her husband—which I didn't remember being—and then, after a moment, I made him in love with someone else. The story picked itself up and headed off on its own two legs. It had become fiction, and I was just along for the ride, interested now that I didn't know what was going to happen. It turned into a tiny novel called *An Actual Life*. It was the easiest thing I ever wrote, and for some reason, a lot of fun. Maybe adding humor and hope to the mix felt like a do-over. As for college? I never went back.

In Which I Repeat Myself

THE MOST IMPORTANT THING WRITING has taught me is this: the more vulnerable you allow yourself to be, the stronger you become. It sounds counterintuitive, I know. It sounds like bullshit. Here's the thing: you can't change the past, but if you can face it, both the present and the future will shift. And it's a hell of a lot easier than wasting your energy keeping something underground. When you drag the shameful thing out of the dark, its power lessens. It is finite. It has edges. You look at it in the light, and in the light you write it down, and in the writing you may find a way to forgive yourself, and in the telling you grow stronger because you have made something new out of it, you have given it shape and meaning.

So when you write about your life, don't skip over the hard parts. What would be the point? Who would you be fooling? Yourself? Oh, please. I learned this the hard way, so stricken with shame that I needed to find a way out. My husband was hit by a car, and he was left with a traumatic brain injury so severe he could not live at home. He was taken to a facility in upstate New York. Once a week I drove up to see him, but it felt so infrequent and so short were the visits that I sold my apartment in the city and bought a house nearby and slowly I began to put a life together. I made new friends, I had a yard where my dogs could run free, I was writing and teaching. Sometimes I was able to bring my husband home for an afternoon. I began to love my new life. But we have a habit of sabotaging ourselves, especially when things are going well, and one day I asked myself if I could wave a wand and change the past, if I could erase my husband's tragic accident, would I? Of course I would, wouldn't I? But I hesitated, and what followed was a terrible confusion of sorrow and shame—this new life had been born of my husband's tragedy.

I needed to write about that shame, hoping for some kind of forgiveness, hoping for clarity, but it was going nowhere. So I did what I always do when confronted by something I can't put to rest, can't find words for, can't bear to know about myself. I took down my *Dictionary of Indo-European Roots*, because sometimes the DNA of a word answers a question you didn't know to ask. I looked up "shame," and I looked up "guilt," but found nothing to enlighten me. Finally I looked up "acceptance." And among the words that acceptance evolved from is one that meant "a thread used in weaving." And in that moment my whole life changed. I understood. Acceptance. Maybe the thread frays, maybe it breaks, but you have to weave it in and then you have to keep on weaving.

Some years later a woman wrote to tell me she had spent a lifetime overwhelmed by guilt over something she had either done or failed to do, until she came across what I'd written. "I used to feel like the worst person on earth," she wrote, "and now I just feel human." Tell the hard truths, clear your vision, be of use.

Outsider Art Writing

OUT OF THE SLUSH PILE at the Viking Press in 1979 came a handwritten manuscript whose first sentence I have never forgotten. It had all the naïve beauty of outsider art, and it's the only written equivalent I've ever come across. The story wasn't publishable, but that sentence has stuck with me. It returns every now and then out of nowhere. "Long, long ago, in the deep deep part of the Atlantic Ocean, there lived and was born the most beautiful fishies of them all." Kills me every time.

So Get Busy

WHO ARE WE? We are mothers, fathers, sons, and daughters, sisters, brothers. We are plumbers, lawyers, homemakers. We have waited tables, we have worked in hospitals. We are masons and secretaries and middle managers and bank tellers. We have sold books, we have sold shoes, we have managed produce departments in big supermarkets, we are engineers and soldiers and police and musicians and scientists. We are teachers. We are comedians and volunteers. We are executives, customer service representatives, carpenters, clerks, babysitters, writers, editors, fishermen, inventors. We have worn high heels and construction boots and gray suits and overalls and pocket protectors.

We have spoken from experience, we have talked through our hats. We have been thanked, we have been humiliated, we have gossiped and worried and gone to bed hungry for one thing or another. We have been paranoid, we have had faith. We have been unfairly blamed, we have been unjustly praised, we have protested and we have kept our mouths shut. We have bragged and we have sold ourselves short. We have believed lies, hidden our feelings, scrutinized our motives. We have followed every lead, we have turned our faces away. We have been generous to a fault, we have guarded our treasures. We have gone out on a limb and we have stayed on the porch.

We are full of contradiction and conflict; we have played different roles at different times (or simultaneously); we have evolved out of many different selves. Writing memoir is one way to explore how you became the person you are. It's the story of how you got here from there. Believe me. It's a good story.

Acknowledgments

I HAVE SO MANY PEOPLE TO THANK. First, my four kids, Sarah, Jennifer, Ralph, and Catherine, thank you for being who you are. Thank you to my sister Eliza and my daughter Catherine who patiently read version after version of these pieces, always helpful and willing and patient. Linda Gravenson, Ann Patty, Craig Mawhirt, Adele Clement-Wilson, and Karen Braziller helped in myriad ways. Thank you all. The indispensable Carol Ebbecke took out a very fine toothed comb when almost all was done. My daughter Jennifer took the jacket photo, thank you, Jen. A thousand thanks belong to the Golden Notebook bookstore in Woodstock and James Conrad, who offered to make these pages into a book and then did so: a hell of a big job, a miracle. Thank you to the writers in my Monday and Thursday workshops who inspire me every week. And my old pal Chuck, for all those years of friendship, there's no way I can thank you enough.